A Lookback at Harrow
150 years in stories and pictures

Don Walter

Inspired by the long-running Harrow Observer series

For
Jake Bahari Modaresi

Production and design: Tracey Bohane/Marianne Reeve

© Don Walter 1995

ISBN 0 9518823 9 2

Published by Orpheus Publications Limited,
7 St John's Road, Harrow, Middlesex HA1 2EE.
Tel: 0181-863 4040 Fax: 0181 424 9945.

Printed and bound in Great Britain by BAS Printers Limited.

No part of this book may be reproduced or transmitted in any form or by any means, electronic, mechanical, photocopying, recording, or otherwise, without prior written permission from the publisher.

Contents

About This Book...5

The Coming of the Railway................................7

From Farms to Homes......................................23

When the Roads were Empty...........................43

A Good Place to Work......................................51

Harrow's Other Schools...................................65

Shops and Shopping 79

A Great Night Out 101

No Half Measures 115

Giving Praise..131

Sporting Traditions 149

Raising the Alarm..163

In Sickness and in Health..............................175

Going Downhill..183

Royal Occasions 191

Index 203

About This Book

With the publication of this book, the Lookback concept achieves its third - and, in many ways, most rewarding - incarnation.

As many readers may remember, the idea of looking back at various aspects of our community life over the past century was first developed as a series of features in the Harrow Observer, (to which the present author was privileged to contribute well over 100 separate pieces).

It then became a large-scale pictorial exhibition, jointly sponsored by the Observer and Kodak Limited, which for some 18 months toured important venues in the Borough.

Finally - and very much in response to public demand - it has now been extended and expanded to create this volume which is neither a picture book nor a detailed Harrow history, but something (we hope entertainingly) in-between.

That much of its pictorial content has never previously been seen in print is due not so much to the diligence of the author as to the generosity of the many friends who have loaned material.

In this context, especial thanks are owed to Sheena Crawley, Editor of the Harrow Observer, for the freedom of the paper's archives and to Bob Thomson, Helen Shorter and the staff of the Harrow Local History Collection at the Harrow Civic Centre Library. It should go on record that their untiring efforts deserve the gratitude not just of the writer but of the whole community of Harrow.

The Coming of the Railway

1. One of the very first trains puffs past Harrow Hill (top right) in this engraving from 1839, now in the Harrow Local History Collection.

For all that there has been a community on Harrow Hill from the time of William The Conqueror's Domesday Book of 1086 – and possibly well before – the coming of the railroad in the 1830s did more to accelerate the growth of what we now know as Harrow than any other single event in its history.

Yet the initial local response to the very first line through Harrow – the original London to Birmingham railway – was far from encouraging. For a start, most of Middlesex was then a highly agricultural area, noted especially for the quality of its hay. Not surprisingly, farmers were worried that the railway would bring in cheaper produce from other areas and thus depress local prices. They also foresaw an end to the profitable use of horses although, in fact, the railway company proved to be a major employer of horses in the transit and delivery of rail-borne goods.

Many local landowners, too, were initially hostile to the alien idea of 'iron horses' racing across their fields although, in a remarkably short space of time, money was to silence most of their criticisms. Lord Northwick, the Lord of the Manor, for example, not only took shares in the company in exchange for his Manorial rights over the land, he also received £3,600 – a huge sum in those days – for the sale of just 17 acres.

The Vicar of Harrow, the Reverend John Cunningham, by contrast, sold the railway more than 30 acres and got a comparatively miserly £210. Nor was he successful in persuading the railway company to abandon all thought of Sunday travel although, for some years, a so-called 'Sunday Break' was observed during the hours at which church services were traditionally held.

Harrow School also expressed various reservations, not least about the location of the first Harrow station on the site of our present Harrow and Wealdstone. The School, it seems, would have preferred a station closer to London on the Wembley side.

The Harrow boys were also apt to get into fights with the gangs of navvies engaged in construction work. According to the Reverend Torre's book of contemporary reminiscences: "The stalwart navvies, many of whom passed through the town to buy baccy and beer... rarely escaped a stone from one of the Harrow boys and their language and bearing, being consequently uncourteous to us, they came to be considered our natural

2. Harrow & Wealdstone Station approach some time before its 1911 rebuilding. The actual station can just be glimpsed behind the women on the far right.

3. An early 1900s portrait of some of the people who kept Harrow and Wealdstone Station running, including station staff, cabbies and omnibus drivers. In those days trains were often held until regular passengers turned up!

4. Hatch End Station, undated but, from the clothes of the waiting passenger, photographed c.1897 when the station, originally called Pinner, first took Hatch End into its name.

enemies". He recalls, in particular, a fist fight which left many spots of blood on the white railings outside the Head Master's House "which blood did not proceed from the boys".

Once the trains were actually in service, resentment and suspicion invariably turned to excitement. A typical response was that of Harrow master, the Reverend A.G. Phelps, who confided to his diary that it was "a great diversion to go down to the railway station and see the arrival of a train". Before long, however, dissatisfaction was being expressed at the rising cost of railway travel. An 1838 fares increase actually prompted a "Memorial from the inhabitants of Harrow for a reduction of the fares" – although it failed to carry any influence.

That same year also witnessed the first local railway fatality, when an employee called Thomas Port slipped between two carriages while collecting excess fares. (Even then, it was not unknown for a passenger to buy a second class ticket, and take a first class seat!) Port's gravestone can still be seen near the front porch

5. At the beginning of the century, trains at Harrow and Wealdstone were met by this privately-operated horse omnibus which ran as far as Bushey.

6. The same station shortly after its rebuilding between 1911 and 1912 to designs by Gerald Horsley, also responsible for the more picturesque - and now listed - Hatch End Station.

of St. Mary's, Harrow on the Hill. As well as a singularly grisly verse recording the peculiarly bloody circumstances of his death, it bears a somewhat ambiguous inscription. For years this prompted the view that he was a hat manufacturer from Burton-on-Trent and so typical of the early well-to-do business traveller. In fact, the hat manufacturer was the dead man's father who apparently paid for the tomb. Poor Thomas thus seems to have been as much a victim of early Victorian snobbery as of Victorian progress.

Once begun, that progress was truly unstoppable. Within three decades the Metropolitan Railway had pioneered underground travel in London. It was then only a matter of time before links were sought with the fast-growing townships around the Metropolis and, by 1880, the extension line from Baker Street had reached Harrow.

This notable landmark in local history was duly celebrated with a buffet lunch for 250 guests at the King's Head Hotel on Harrow Hill, still the true centre of the town; indeed, the principal entrance to the first Metropolitan station was built on the Hill side. Here, for generations (certainly into the 1920s), trains would be met by a line of horse-drawn cabs. Moreover, although originally called Harrow, this down-the-hill station was in 1894 given the name it retains to this day – Harrow on the Hill.

Ten years later, another new line opened to Stanmore, largely at the instigation of an entrepreneur called Frederick Gordon. Having purchased the vast mansion of Bentley Priory and turned it into an hotel, Gordon decided that business would be improved by better communications and so invested much of his fortune into a single-track line. This was formally opened with a lunch at Bentley Priory on December 18th, 1890 and – according to our local railway enthusiast, Peter G Scott – the first train to Stanmore left Harrow at 12.17p.m. that day.

The Great Stanmore Parish Council were initially – and understandably – concerned about

7. A pair of Leyland motor buses wait at Harrow and Wealdstone's Marlborough Road entrance when it served as a bus terminus around 1912.

8. To enable passengers to get from one platform to another the first Metropolitan station at Harrow – seen here in 1921 – had a tunnel beneath the tracks.

the prospect of a station in their somewhat exclusive area and, at their insistence, the building that ultimately arose had more the appearance of a Victorian Gothic Church than a railway terminal. Much converted, and now a private home, it still stands in Gordon Avenue, named after the line's principal founder. The line had one intermediate station at Belmont which (like Stanmore Station itself) finally closed in 1964.

A new century had begun before the other (South) side of the town had a station of its own. This was South Harrow, opened in 1903 as part of the extension of the newly electrified District Line. Offering easy access to Earl's Court, Kensington and the West End shops, it quickly proved popular with passengers, although the use of the name South Harrow rather than the older Roxeth provoked considerable criticism. To this day, many locals sincerely believe that this one simple act planted the seed for the downfall of Roxeth, which had been the accepted name for the area for close on 1000 years.

Clarke & Co., the estate agents, even felt obliged to describe the location of South Harrow when compiling a catalogue for the auction of 70 building plots on the nearby Mount Park Estate. It was, they said, "that portion of the singularly favourite town of Harrow occupying the picturesque South and South West slopes of the Harrow Hill". More intriguingly, they added that "being amply protected by nature from the North and East winds, South Harrow is always several degrees warmer than any of the surrounding districts".

Though the first South Harrow station was replaced in 1935 by a new and bigger station in Northolt Road, the original building still remains just a few 100 yards up South Hill Avenue. To our eyes, it looks more like a house than a station and, in the earliest days, it actually provided a home for the station master and his wife – not that they were always at home! According to "Harrow Before Your Time", that wonderful collection of local memories, the wife was more than fond of a drink and, on Saturday

9. Earlier this century a large pointing finger (right middle distance) showed the way to the Metropolitan Railway's College Road entrance.

10. A similar directional sign was also erected near the railway bridge in Station Road. Eighty years later, many of these buildings still survive.

11. Since so many of its early passengers lived on Harrow Hill the original Metropolitan Station had this imposing entrance on the Lowlands Road side.

nights, she and her dog would make their way to "The Three Horseshoes" in Northolt Road. Here she was apt to shed her clothing until the well-timed arrival of the Constable from West Street police station who would solemnly trundle her to the cells on a little hand-pushed cart, a procedure that would hardly be practicable in the traffic-ridden South Harrow of today.

12. Harrow on the Hill Station as it looked in 1933, a few years after the opening of the Embassy Cinema whose advertising can be seen on the far platform.

13. It looks very much like a rural halt on a country line - in fact, it is Northwick Park Station photographed in the summer of 1930.

14. The entrance to North Harrow Station as it was in 1933 when the bridge across Imperial Drive was advertising semi-detached houses for £850.

15. *The original District Line Underground Station at South Harrow around 1903 when it also served as the station master's home.*

16. *Although South Harrow had grown sufficiently to justify a railway station, South Hill Avenue still presented a tranquil appearance in the early 1900s.*

17. Original signage for the District Station, opened in June 1903, carried the words "South Harrow for Roxeth and Northolt": the last four words were later dropped.

19. Like the original South Harrow Station, the first Alperton Station was of modest size and construction. It was rebuilt in 1931 and a bus garage erected on the adjoining land.

18. In 1935 South Harrow had a brand-new station built to the high design standards then winning widespread acclaim for London Transport's architects.

20. Opened in 1932 Belmont Halt was the only intermediate station on the single-track Harrow and Stanmore line. It finally closed after some 32 years.

21. The end of the line - Stanmore Village Station prior to its demolition in July 1970.

From Farms to Homes

1. Harrow Weald's rural past is vividly evoked by this picture of shepherd, flock and dog in the yard of Weald Farm, once situated on the corner of Weald Lane and High Road.

Older townsfolk are often heard to comment that "it used to be all fields around here".

What gives the remark a particular poignancy when heard in Harrow is that the speaker need be nowhere near as old as the century. Local people born as late as the 1930s will vividly recall the country walks they could take in many parts of Harrow, although, even then, the green fields and farms were beginning to be swallowed up by the red brick of present-day suburbia.

2. Honeybun Farm, off Bessborough Road, was already picturesquely old when this undated picture was taken. It later gave way to council housing.

Until that time, 'development', had tended to be in isolated clumps rather than continuous ribbons. The opening of railway stations at Harrow & Wealdstone, Harrow On The Hill and South Harrow, for instance, caused considerable development in their immediate vicinity. There was also the inescapable fact that the narrow ridge of Harrow Hill prevented any real expansion of the original hill-top town so virtually all the main facilities and services were obliged either to move permanently downhill or, at least, to open additional branches on the lower ground.

Soon, with the promise of easy access to the London job market on one side and genuine countryside on the other, Harrow was poised for major expansion. Among the builders quick to seize this opportunity was T.F. Nash who, from registered offices in Eastcote Lane, South Harrow, built up one of the most successful building companies in Britain. In 1925, just three years after setting up business, Nash began on his huge Kenton project which ultimately grew into a veritable township comprising some 2,200 houses and shops off Kenton Road between St. Leonard's Avenue and Kenton Park Avenue.

3. Rayners Farm, at one time part-owned by the Hall family of Roxeth Farm, was acquired for development in 1928 by Metropolitan Railway Country Estates.

4. Durrants Farm, whose name lives on in today's Durrants Court, in High Road, Harrow Weald, was the farm to which the family of novelist Anthony Trollope moved when they fell upon hard times.

Eight years later, he turned his attention to the Rayners Lane area. A handsome colour brochure produced for the firm in 1933 proudly speaks of nearly 1,000 homes completed and a further 3,500 homes, shops and other facilities being built, including, as it proved, Rayners Lane's architecturally renowned Grosvenor Cinema.

At this time, Nash was able to claim a totally integrated operation with its own vast joinery works in Wealdstone, a substantial heavy transport fleet, even a spacious Nash garage to house the many modern automobiles in which prospective buyers were shown around the estates.

By the mid-1930s the company was confident enough to stage a Grand Shopping Week for would-be buyers. Special features included a triumphal arch suspended across Alexandra Avenue, firework displays and the offer of cheap evening rail tickets on the Metropolitan and Piccadilly lines. (A monthly Rayners Lane to Aldgate ticket was then the equivalent of £1.70.)

Nash believed strongly in the impact of advertising and, wherever one looked, there

5. Although sometimes called Roxeth Farm, this rambling old building in Northolt Road, (where Sainsburys now stands) was better known as Barnett's Farm.

6. *Headstone Manor photographed between the two World Wars when it was still a working concern known as Moat Farm.*

7. *Damaged during World War II, the Great Barn of Roxeth was pulled down a few years later, despite being one of the finest structures of its kind in the county.*

seemed to be notices for Nash properties featuring the powerful assurance that "£25 deposit secures". In any event, Nash Homes were going at that time for around £595-£615 for a 3-bedroomed terraced property or £750 for a 4-bedroom semi, complete with integral garage.

Those Harrow properties that were not Nash-built were highly likely to be the work of one of three other local companies. One was E.S. Reed who, at one time, lived in one of his own houses in Northumberland Road, and went on to develop the popular Harrow Garden Village, north of Rayners Lane station, for the Metropolitan Railway Company Country Estates Limited. The other well-remembered names are Alfred Cutler and Sons, who built extensively in and around Pinner Road, and Frederick and Charles Costain, whose company was responsible for much of the south side of Kenton.

Laing Estates and Harry Neal also made a considerable contribution to Harrow's housing, the latter diversifying into public buildings that included Harrow's first open-air swimming pool in Charles Crescent, the Northwood, Pinner and District Hospital and the massive Gaumont State Cinema at Kilburn.

Meanwhile, across the border in present day Brent, similar entrepreneurial skills were being demonstrated by yet another local resident, James Comben. When he died in 1931, his obituary in the Harrow Observer declared (with no pun intended), that his was "a household name amongst all classes of the community". The writer also estimated that his firm of Comben and Wakeling had, in fact, housed nearly one-third of Wembley's population.

8. Around the turn of the century, children pose by a signpost at what appears to be the junction of today's Watford Road and Sudbury Court Road.

9. Though the name still survives, Grange Road, off Northolt Road, South Harrow, has lost all the old cottages and the corner shop seen in this evocative early 20th century picture.

10. By 1906 the first shops and houses have appeared on one side of Northolt Road but fields still remain opposite. The tent belonged to the Baptist Mission.

11. Around 1912, children flock to "The Paddocks", a private sports ground and amusement centre in Northolt Road.

12. Another pre-World War I view of Northolt Road looking towards the recently-built railway bridge from outside the gas works.

13. The open fields of Roxeth as seen from the air in the early 1920's. The road, running from top right to centre foreground crossed by the railway, is Northolt Road.

14. A view of Kenton Lane showing some of the farm land which remained in the possession of New College, Oxford from its 1504 endowment to the early 1930s.

15. Elm Park, Stanmore, as it looked around 1920, when it was described as "a wide road of gravel and grass with dog-roses growing down each side".

16. Stanmore is another area that has grown almost beyond recognition. This, for example, is London Road around the turn of the century showing the old village pond on the left and a property called The Red House on the right.

17. The Old Berkeley Hunt was still meeting in Stanmore in the early 1930s although the fast growth of suburbia meant its days were already numbered.

18. Honeypot Lane, Stanmore, as it looked some 65 years ago.

19. In May 1929, walkers follow the public footpath that led from College Hill Road to Byron Road, Wealdstone.

20. An idyllic view of Rayners Lane as it looked in the early 1920s. It was named after the Rayners whose farm was the only building there throughout the 19th century.

21. This tranquil scene in Rayners Lane was soon to change for the noticeboard heralds a 'New Station' offering frequent services to London.

22. When photographed in September 1929, Rayners Lane railway bridge and the small station ticket office were almost totally surrounded by fields.

23. The junction of Pinner Road and Headstone Lane some time between 1920 and 1925 when the hoarding promised the "Finest Labour-Saving Homes In The District", from £850.

24. Rayners Lane (where Whittington Way and Suffolk Road meet today) as it was in 1932. The sign points across the fields to North Harrow Station.

25. *The entrance to the Nash Estate in Alexandra Avenue, Rayners Lane, as it appeared in the great home-building year of 1937.*

26. *As late as 1937 there was still land available off Headstone Drive to allow Kodak Ltd to build a new Stock and Shipping Department.*

27. By 1936, when extensive work was done on the Rayners Lane railway bridge, the ticket office carried an advertisement for T.F. Nash whose homes were already appearing on the skyline.

28. An undated but possibly turn of the century picture taken in Douglas Avenue, Wembley. The sign for J.W. Comben, the local builder, offered homes from only £250.

29. World War I was still some seven years away when Marie Gunn and her friends were photographed on Belmont Common. Later, Marie (whose father kept the Duck in the Pond) recalled that the photographer had provided the picturesque bonnets and smocks.

When the Roads were Empty

1. Police and passers-by collect around the Daimler Wagonette after its tragic 1899 accident at the foot of Grove Hill. The car's collapsed back wheel can be clearly seen.

As hundreds of concrete front gardens testify, much of present day Harrow was built at a time when ownership of a motor car was the privilege of only a relatively few enthusiasts: indeed, 100 years ago, the merest glimpse of a car in our streets was considered fully worthy of comment in the local press.

In the Harrow Gazette of August 8th 1896, for example, we can read how "the progress through the streets" of a car leaving Harrow for Windsor was "watched with most interest". Then, just three weeks later, the same paper reported that "a second car passed through

2. Unveiled in 1969, this wall-mounted plaque at the top of Grove Hill commemorates the fatal accident that happened 70 years before.

Harrow and on it we noticed Mr. Thomas, the general manager of Wembley Park".

From then on, the theme of who owned what was to be steadily developed and in August, 1902, Dr. Joseph Wood, Head Master of Harrow School, was identified "as the latest motor enthusiast". Dr. Wood, it seems, had just taken possession of "a magnificent six-horsepower DeDion Bouton phaeton", which further impressed the reporter by being custom-built.

Harrow's greatest motoring buff, however, was undoubtedly the celebrated librettist, W.S. Gilbert, then living in some splendour at Grim's Dyke, Harrow Weald. Here he kept a succession of cars (often several at a time) beginning with an American Locomobile steam-car.

It has to be said that Gilbert was probably not the safest of drivers and, in private correspondence, he admitted "spoiling a parson who came round from under a dead wall on a bicycle". On this occasion, Mrs Gilbert had been "pitched very comfortably into a hedge where she looked like a large and unaccountable bird's nest".

Though Gilbert, the humorist, could afford to laugh, Gilbert, the magistrate and Deputy Lieutenant for Middlesex, had to proceed with greater caution and a suitable chauffeur was soon employed at Grim's Dyke. Nevertheless it is tempting to speculate that it might have been Gilbert at the wheel when, that same year, a local lady reported seeing her first car "somewhat erratically steered" in Harrow Weald Common Road. The lady was pushing a pram at the time, and felt obliged to take the baby "off the road and on to the common for safety".

Evasive pedestrian action may have been even more essential on some of Harrow's steeper hills. As early as December 1896, a motor car was reported driving up Sudbury Hill "when it became uncontrollable and ran back into a ditch".

3. When taken on a trial run in this type of L.N.W.R. omnibus in July 1906, the local press claimed "there can be no prettier route than its Wealdstone to Watford run".

4. An early L.N.W.R. omnibus bound for Watford Station chugs along the remarkably little changed High Street, Harrow on the Hill, some 80 years ago.

Then, in 1899, a genuine tragedy occurred on Grove Hill, all the sadder for the fact that the journey had begun in particularly happy circumstances. The car concerned was an 8-seater Daimler Wagonette and its driver and passengers were all connected with the famous Army and Navy Stores, apparently contemplating the regular use of such vehicles as an alternative to rail delivery. What more natural then that Samuel Greenhill, manager of the Carriage Department and a Harrow resident, should suggest a test run from London to Harrow, where the party duly took tea at the King's Head Hotel.

Unfortunately, Edwin Sewell, the driver, braked too hard on the descent of Grove Hill and the car overturned. All the occupants were thrown into the roadway, and Sewell and, subsequently, Major Riches died from the injuries they received.

5. Route 58 buses waiting outside The Seven Balls in Kenton Lane around 1912. These early solid-tyre vehicles were operated by the London General Omnibus Co., forerunner of London Transport.

6. Even in the early 1920s a Red Cross truck is the only vehicle visible from outside the Crown Inn in Church Road, Stanmore.

7. In the 1906 election, when he contested the Harrow Division, the Hon. W. Peek found that a motor was a sure way to win both attention and votes!

For some strange reason, a plaque commemorating the accident was erected only in 1969 - and then on a wall at the top of the Hill rather than at the bottom where the accident occurred. Nor is its version of the accident entirely correct. It was not, as it states, the first recorded motor accident involving the death of the driver. (That dubious distinction fell to one Henry Lindfield of Brighton who died after his Imperial Electric Carriage had crashed in February, 1898). It was, however, the first fatality in a petrol-driven car and also the first to involve the death of a passenger.

Edwin Sewell had apparently been one of the country's very first motorists, and his son complained bitterly that the plaque made no mention of the pioneering aspects of his career. Further controversy arose about the identity of the passerby bold enough to switch off the car's ignition following the crash. Lord Brabazon of Tara who, at the time, was a 14-year-old pupil of Harrow School, subsequently claimed this distinction in his autobiography. This, however,

8. With boiling radiator, a Watford-bound open-top bus makes heavy weather of the ascent of Stanmore Hill around 1913, when the service first began.

9. Around the same period, another 142 passes The Vine, Stanmore and, possibly, one of its departing customers.

10. Prior to the automobile, the tricycle was a popular way to take to the road - as here in Church Lane, Pinner.

was subsequently challenged in the local press by a lady writing from Canada to the effect that the task had been performed by her father, then proprietor of a nearby shop.

A happier footnote was added in the mid-1970s when a picture of the accident was published in the magazine "Country Life". Lord Greenhill of Harrow (the former career diplomat Denis Arthur Greenhill and grandson of the Greenhill who had organised the original outing) wrote that family tradition insisted that his grandfather's life had been saved by the fact that he always wore the next best thing to a crash helmet - a sturdy old-fashioned top hat!

For all the early interest in the motor car, the horse was still a long way from being replaced although, at a local Council meeting in April 1910, some dissatisfaction was expressed at the quality of the horses employed. One Councillor declared that the Horse Committee was such a poor judge of horse flesh that the Council was "the laughing stock of the town in the matter of their horses".

Another then raised the matter of "motor traction". He was firmly quashed, a Councillor Strickland remarking that with regard to the motor "owing to the nature of the district and the class of work they had to do, it would be a long time before anything came of that idea".

A Good Place to Work

1. Kodak's Harrow staff in 1891, taken from a photograph printed on the first-ever Harrow-coated celluloid film.

The coming of the railway to Harrow was seemingly welcomed and excoriated in almost equal measure, but neither its greatest advocate nor its toughest critic could have foreseen quite the impact it would eventually have upon the whole community, not least in the provision of work.

Not only did the railway create new jobs in itself, the new and relatively easy communications it provided brought many manufacturing companies to the district.

Whereas only 150 years ago, working in Harrow almost certainly meant a job on the land or in some allied craft, a place in service or in trade, the last decades of the 19th century offered a whole new range of opportunities in

2. An evocative glimpse of the Harrow factory's laboratory shortly after the opening when stiff white collars seem to have been the required form of dress.

the many factories that sprang up around the first local station, the present Harrow and Wealdstone. Whitefriars Glass Works, Hamilton's Brush Works and Winsor and Newton, suppliers of artists' materials, all built substantial bases – and reputations – in Wealdstone. The one unfortunate exception appears to have been the gunsmiths, Cogswell and Harrison, for whom proximity to the railway proved a disaster rather than a blessing. In 1894, a spark from a passing steam engine is said to have ignited a truly calamitous blaze.

Two years later, a Belfast-based publishing company, David Allen & Sons, built an elaborate printing works in Headstone Drive with a vast 170ft power-house chimney on which the company name was emblazoned in giant letters.

Although their special expertise was in the production of the spectacular pictorial posters then used by London's major theatres, they quickly gained a reputation as one of the best all-round lithographic printers in the country or, for that

3. In the 1890s women check chemical materials in the clean, bright surroundings for which Kodak was already well known.

4. Women were also employed in the photo-packing room. From the variety of apron styles, they probably wore their own.

matter, Europe. Indeed, when World War I broke out, the Government – having, they said, looked at some 200 other firms – took over the Wealdstone firm to produce ration books, official leaflets and all the other requirements of wartime publicity and propaganda.

Not surprisingly, the company felt that substantial compensation was their due. To negotiate with the Government on their behalf they hired the noted Ulster lawyer, Sir Edward Carson, who had prosecuted Oscar Wilde at his trials. Carson evidently earned his fees for he ultimately secured some £315,000 from the Old Harrovian Stanley Baldwin, then Financial Secretary to the Treasury. In 1920, the Allen printing works officially became His Majesty's Stationery Office, a role which they continued to fill right up until the 1980s.

An even more famous early arrival was George Eastman's American-based Kodak company which, in 1890, bought for its first overseas operation some seven acres of Wealdstone land. The Kodak name was then only two years old, having been dreamed up by Eastman himself in his search for a brand that could be spelled and pronounced without difficulty in any country in the world.

As it proved, these world-wide ambitions were soon to be realised and the original seven

5. *The very epitome of well-dressed Edwardian manhood - branch managers on a visit to Kodak in March, 1907.*

6. Loading up for a delivery in 1904, possibly to one of the retail shops already existing at Cheapside, Regent Street and Oxford Street.

7. Kodak staff swarm around the gates in this undated shot which, judging from the women's cloche hats, was taken in the mid-1920s.

8. Another shot of the Kodak gates from the same era. It was possibly taken at the lunch break since the clock in the distance reads 12 o'clock.

acres in Wealdstone subsequently increased to 55, holding some 100 buildings with a workforce many thousands strong; in fact, for many years, the largest private employer in the district.

Since scrupulous cleanliness was essential to the work – and clean air had been a deciding factor in the decision to move to Harrow – the Kodak factory was, from the very start, an exceptionally clean and inviting place in which to work.

Unusually for the period, a great variety of jobs were open to women and, soon, girls from various parts of Harrow were to be seen walking across the fields to Kodak. A particular loser was the Harrow School Laundry in South Harrow but, then, there was scarcely a period in its history when this sizeable local employer was not without staffing problems. One can still read at the Civic Centre Library the rueful comment of the Laundry Committee's chairman, the Rev. A.G. Watson, that, since the laundry's opening, "it has been found necessary to change all the heads of department, the Manageress once, the Engineer three times, the Foreman of the Wash-house

9. The imposing Victorian entrance to the printing works of David Allen & Sons, later His Majesty's Stationery Office, in Headstone Drive.

10. Inside the printing works around the same period, showing several striking posters in the course of production.

11. *Another view of the interior of David Allen's taken shortly after its opening in 1896.*

three times and the Forewoman of Ironers three times". Nevertheless, for all its problems, he still felt that a school laundry was far preferable to the earlier practice of having the schoolboys' clothes put at the mercy of "reckless and irresponsible washerwomen".

In complete contrast, Miss E.B. Jayne, who ran the highly successful Little Laundry in Stuart Road, Wealdstone, seems to have been what might now be termed an outstanding people manager. When World War I began, Lloyd George, then Minister of Munitions, gave her the job of recruiting, organising and controlling the women required to maintain the wartime munitions factories. Later, a grateful country gave her an O.B.E.

Another major employer in old Roxeth was the still-remembered gas works in Northolt Road, whose rapid development reflected the widespread use of gas following its local introduction in 1855.

From modest beginnings on a one-and-three-quarter acre site, (celebrated by a King's Head dinner at which the chandeliers were lit by "the new illuminant"), the gas works finally spread over some 15 acres. Later, it created enormous controversy when, at the end of the 1920s, it

12. *Miss E.B. Jayne outside her Little Laundry premises in Stuart Road, Wealdstone, with the pony and trap in which, prior to World War I, she regularly drove from her Stanmore home.*

13. *Even when it grew in size, the Little Laundry was reluctant to change its name which - in the form of Little and Good - was ideal for advertising purposes.*

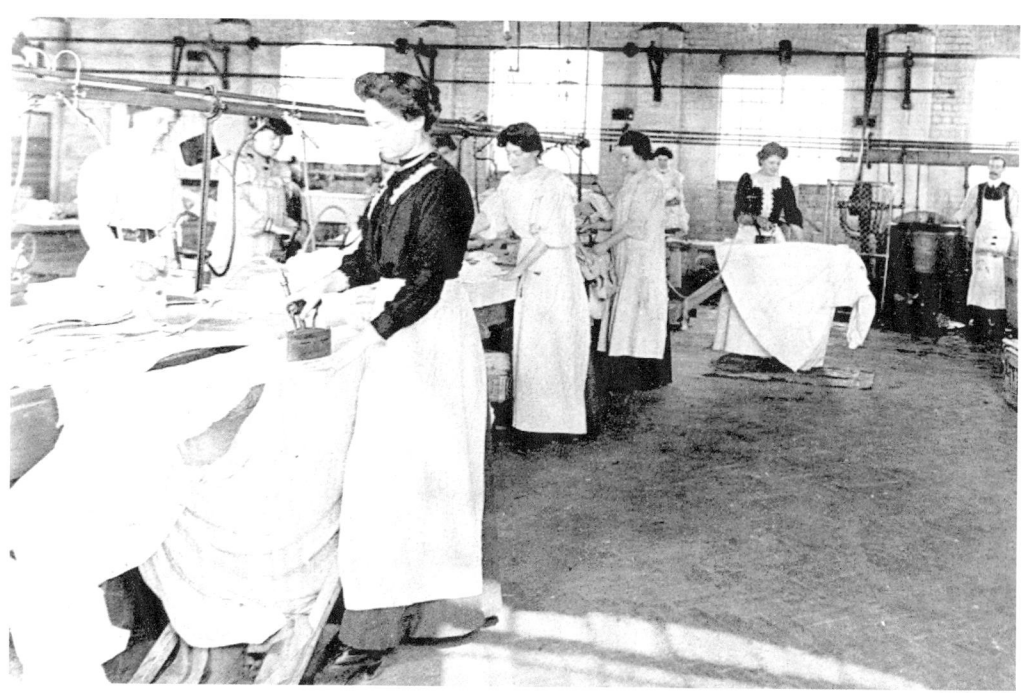

14. Voluminous Edwardian fashions meant that there was a lot of pressing to be done - on the heavy gas irons of the day.

was decided to build a gas holder 240ft high, 162ft in diameter with a 4 million cubic foot capacity.

Though some attempt was made at camouflage during World War II, the holder effectively dominated the local sky-line, not least because of the massive 'NO' painted on its side. No-one seems certain whether this was intended as shorthand for nearby Northolt Airport or just a simple negative; either way, its presence was rendered necessary by an extraordinary incident in which the pilot of a large commercial aircraft apparently confused the Roxeth holder with the one at Southall and put down at Northolt Airport rather than his proper destination at Heathrow.

For all their size, the buildings of the gas works have now vanished as completely as The Three Horseshoes, the little public house next door, over whose side wall many a gas worker regularly climbed to enjoy a forbidden lunch-time drink.

One relic of Roxeth's more industrial past does remain – the surprisingly attractive Laundry Superintendent's House designed by the noted architect E.S. Prior as part of the Harrow School Laundry complex. Though somewhat overshadowed by modern housing developments, it is

15. A typical scene in the packing room of the firm which later became Advance Contract Laundries with contracts from major London hotels.

16. For most of this century, Roxeth Gas Works in Northolt Road, South Harrow presented a lively scene of activity.

17. *Now demolished, the Roxeth gas holder dominated the scene for much of this century. The 'NO' was presumed to identify nearby Northolt Airport.*

still worth a detour down Grange Road, if you ever find yourself at the Hill end of Northolt Road.

Those with a feeling for the town's industrial past might also care to visit Old Redding at Harrow Weald to see the single cottage now remaining from the once-famous development known as "The City", in effect, one of the first 'estates' anywhere in the country to be built by a paternalistic employer for his work-force.

The man in question was Charles Blackwell of Harrow Weald who, some 165 years ago, put up some 14 cottages which, in their heyday, housed around 120 employees of his nearby brick works. At this remove, it is impossible to say how such a modest development acquired such a grandiose name, although the English Place Name Society, the leading authority on the subject, is of the opinion that it began as a deliberate joke which just happened to stick.

In any event, there was a similar degree of jokiness in the re-naming of 'The Case Is Altered', the public house on the opposite side of the road. For most of The City's existence,

18. The Knotts ran a carriage-building business in Wealdstone High Street. Around the turn-of-the-century, it doubled as Wealdstone's fire station.

19. The Nobes family, pictured c.1900, had a successful forge and wheel-wright's business near Roxeth Corner for more than 40 years.

20. A pony and trap passes The City, the Old Redding community of cottages built by Charles Blackwell for the labourers in his brick works.

21. Known as an unusually beneficent employer Thomas Blackwell returned some 15 acres to the parish in 1895 to create Harrow Weald Recreation Ground. In gratitude, the parish erected these gates, which still stand to his memory.

this still-existing establishment was affectionately known as The Cathedral - because, the argument went, any true city had to have a cathedral of its own.

In addition to the one remaining workers' cottage, much evidence of brick-making still survives in the area, notably in the name of Clamp Hill (a clamp being the trade description of a pile of bricks waiting to be fired). The sheer amount of brick clay removed from the area is also said to account for the fact that the land between Brookshill and Clamp Hill is now lower than either road.

Today, anyone tackling the Borough's Bentley Priory Circular Walk can easily break their route to walk the perimeter of the original kiln, now part of The Kiln Nurseries and Garden Centre. On this little detour, you not only pick your way across one-time clay diggings, you also get the occasional glimpse of The Kiln House, the lovely old house that became one of the homes of the Blackwell family.

As shown in Alan Ball's book, "The Countryside Lies Sleeping", The Kiln House features in a particularly attractive painting by Frederick Goodall, the first distinguished owner of nearby Grimsdyke. Called "The Day of Rest At The Old Home", it shows one of the old horses happily 'retired' from the Soho premises of yet another Blackwell business - and major employer. We know it today as Crosse and Blackwell.

Harrow's Other Schools

1. This still-standing block of Roxeth Hill School was built in 1851 as a memorial to the son of the noted philanthropist Lord Shaftesbury.

Having established a home and found a job locally, where did Harrow's people turn for the education of their children?

The answer, at least from the early 19th century, was certainly not to Harrow School which, largely because of its strictly classical Latin-taught curriculum, was already proving uncongenial to local lads destined to follow their fathers into farming or trade.

For all that, there were still many in the parish who felt that local youngsters were being cheated of their "inheritance" and several major protests were mounted, that of 1810

2. Lord Shaftesbury is himself remembered by this plaque on the road up to St. Mary's Church, where he witnessed the pauper's funeral that he later claimed changed his life.

actually taking the school to law. In truth, such protests were not finally silenced until the passing of the Public Schools Act in 1868, which made it wholly legal for such old foundations as Harrow to open their doors to all comers; to become, in the proper sense of the phrase, public schools - albeit open only to those members of the public willing and able to pay the not inconsiderable fees.

In 1811, however, the town was still seething over the failure of its action in the Courts of Chancery, and the new Vicar of Harrow, the Rev. John Cunningham, was quick to see the need for some proper local alternative to John Lyon's Foundation.

Within a year, Cunningham had opened a parish school, probably on London (later Roxeth) Hill, supported by voluntary subscriptions including his own donation of £20, and some £26 he had managed to squeeze from the notoriously tight-fisted Baron Northwick, then Lord of the Manor and Patron of St. Mary's. Even so, the first year's expenses far exceeded the money subscribed and it seems that Cunningham met this – and subsequent shortfalls – from his own pocket.

3. At the still-recognisable Roxeth Corner, c.1908, local school boys assemble in what looks very much their Sunday best - possibly for a parish outing.

4. Hands behind backs, Class Two pose for the photographer shortly after the opening of Welldon Park School, South Harrow, in February 1912.

5. A typically Victorian portrait of Marion Hewlett whose unbounded energies gave rise to technical education in Harrow.

That there was a real need for such a School was amply demonstrated by its rapid growth, a Digest of Parochial Returns for 1816 listing a Day and Sunday School at Harrow with 170 children supported by subscriptions.

Almost 40 years later, towards the end of his 50-year ministry, Cunningham was also largely instrumental in the building that still survives at the heart of Roxeth First and Middle School on Roxeth Hill.

The circumstances of its erection were initially tragic. Anthony Ashley Cooper, the 7th Earl of Shaftesbury and one of the great philanthropists of the Victorian era, had a favourite son at Harrow School. The boy, however, died at 16 while still a pupil and masters and boys quickly raised some £600 for a handsome memorial. Cunningham seems to have persuaded them to put the money instead towards the construction of a new parish school, for which the foundation stone was laid in June 1851.

Known originally as the National Schools and Ashley Memorial, the block still stands - and serves - although an adjoining classroom block, built as recently as 1973, was subsequently demolished as unsafe!

Meanwhile, Charles Vaughan, one of Harrow School's most forward-thinking Head Masters, had opened a so-called English Form in which a limited curriculum was taught in the native tongue for a modest fee. Later, on the recommendation of the Royal Commission that produced the Public Schools Act, this Form acquired its own building in Middle Road, and its own identity as The Lower School of John Lyon, today's still-expanding John Lyon School.

At this time, of course, there were still many who truly believed that girls scarcely required a

6. A rare picture of Isabella Rotch in 1901. Her recurrent dream of a house invaded by girls came true when her home became Harrow Girls County School.

7. *Another view of the old "Harrow Tech" taken some time in the 1920s when there were still private houses next door.*

8. *A mothercare class photographed at Harrow Technical College in 1923.*

9. *Lowlands, the house which gave its name to Lowlands Road, has seen many uses - as a family home, then as the original Harrow Girls' County School and, currently, as part of the vast Greenhill College complex.*

formal education at all, certainly not after the age of 12. This century was already twelve years old before plans were laid for a girls' grammar school on a site in Lowlands Road.

Although Harrow Girls County has long since been absorbed into today's massive Greenhill College, the house where it all began – a graceful white Georgian villa – still stands, perhaps a little incongruously, among the more brutal bulk of later buildings.

Called "Lowlands", a name it subsequently gave to Lowlands Road, the villa was for most of the 19th century the home of Benjamin Rotch, a notably successful barrister, magistrate and MP, and his wife Isabella. Much younger than her husband, Isabella outlived him for more than half a century and, indeed, was still resident at "Lowlands" when she died in 1909. Towards the end of her 100 years, Isabella (who had no children of her own), told Edgar Stogden, then Vicar of Harrow, of a recurrent dream in which she saw her house filled with girls in identical clothing. The dream very quickly came true although the unromantic might say that Isabella actively helped in the

10. *A 19th century picture of the lodge to Lowlands in Lowlands Road. When its owner, Benjamin Rotch, was a magistrate in the 1840s it was used as Harrow's first court house.*

11. *The once-familiar exterior of Greenhill School at the junction of St. Ann's Road and Havelock Place, in Central Harrow.*

12. Many generations passed through the boys department of Greenhill School pictured shortly after its opening in 1896. It closed in the late 1960s.

process by leaving her property to Harrow School. They, in turn, offered it to the county for educational purposes.

Thus, the first girls' grammar school in the district opened its doors in 1913. Much of Mrs. Rotch's land was, however, transformed into the existing Lowlands Recreation Ground since nobody then saw the need for other than a relatively small school.

At this period the facade of "Lowlands" was still decorated with two large stone eagles but these were considered far too aggressive for the gaze of young ladies. Consequently, they were transported up the Hill where they can now be found perched atop the porch of "Bradbys", one of Harrow School's boarding houses in the High Street.

Even without its eagles, "Lowlands" seems to have proved excitingly romantic for its first pupils who, from the discovery of a small room with barred windows, built an amazing story of how the site had once housed prisoners en route to Tyburn – and the gallows. For all that there still exists a stretch

13. Schooldays as many still remember them - an undated but atmospheric picture taken at Grant Road School, Wealdstone, whose junior department opened as early as 1870.

14. Bridge Schools, Wealdstone, occupied the present Civic Centre site for nearly 60 years.

15. Pupils of Bridge Schools entertain the war-wounded on Empire Day, 1917.

of road called Tyburn Lane, just a few yards away, the more prosaic truth is that, during Rotch's years as a magistrate, the house sometimes doubled as a police court, and the room probably served as a holding cell.

It was not just in the provision of academic education that Harrow ultimately excelled. The town was also relatively quick to provide its adult citizens with classes in technical subjects. The impetus here came largely from one woman, the redoubtable Marion Hewlett, daughter of the town's doctor, Thomas Hewlett, and one of those tireless and high-minded Victorians who saw it as their bounden duty to improve the lot of those less fortunately placed.

Having founded the Harrow and Roxeth Dispensary, which provided medicines to those who might otherwise have gone without, Marion decided that the time had come to devote equal attention to their mental well-being.

16. Another celebration of Empire Day at Bridge School, possibly just after World War I.

17. Children make their way to Whitefriars School, Whitefriars Avenue, Wealdstone in 1912, one year after its opening.

In 1887, in a room in Harrow High Street, she started classes "to develop among working boys and girls higher ideals and love of art and science". Happily, these somewhat lofty sentiments did not preclude a healthy streak of practicality. Right from the start there were cookery classes, since Miss Hewlett apparently shared Mrs Beeton's view that "many working class homes are made miserable by bad cooking".

Miss Hewlett was equally convinced of the need for dress-making classes. "It is an undoubted fact", she wrote, "that, in London, thousands of French dressmakers are employed because English women cannot be found competent either to cut out dresses or to fit them correctly".

Already confident of help from Harrow Hill's notables – and who would dare argue with so formidable a lady? – Miss Hewlett sought to bolster it with Royal support, turning to H.R.H. Princess Louise, a distinguished daughter of Queen Victoria. The Princess, who already shared her interest in the animal welfare group known as the Band of Mercy, promptly consented not only to become the

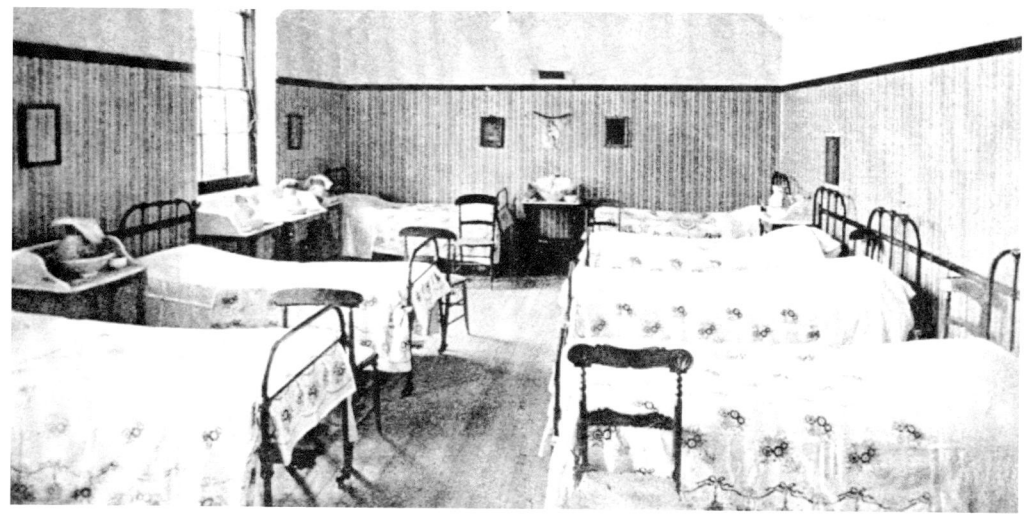

18. The kind of dormitory to be found at Orley Farm School after 1901 when it moved to the building Arnold Mitchell had designed in South Hill Avenue, Harrow.

19. Like many great houses, Stanmore Park survived for a while as a school when its finely proportioned rooms were turned into class-rooms.

20. An art class at the mansion at Bentley Priory when it, too was used as a school earlier this century.

21. The original building of The John Lyon School (formerly the Lower School of John Lyon), still stands in Middle Road.

22. The 19th century part of Roxeth Hill School is now approached by way of an uncompromisingly 20th century footbridge.

school's patron but also to visit the first exhibition of class work.

This exhibition was duly held in May 1889 at 4p.m. – "trusting that it may be a convenient time for the working man and woman" – and its very real success provided exactly the boost Miss Hewlett required for her campaign. Within 12 years, the local newspaper was publishing an architect's drawing of "the new technical school now in course of construction on a site in Station Road, Greenhill".

Countless older residents will still recall with affection the handsome red-brick building that ultimately arose on a site near the junction with St. Ann's Road. There it continued to prosper as the 'local tech' until the late 1950s, when engineering students were the first to lead an exodus to Watford Road. By the early 1970s, the art students, too, had moved to the present complex (currently part of the University of Westminster), whose buildings are now of a size and scale that would have amazed even so ambitious a visionary as Marion Hewlett.

Shops and Shopping

1. Selling and restoring hats and umbrellas, R. Burns (formerly Chathams) was typical of the Harrow High Street stores largely dependent on Harrow School patronage. It was to Burns you turned if you needed a topper blocked or repaired for Ascot and the Eton-Harrow match.

Though some may prefer Watford, and others Ealing, the fact remains that Harrow is, at the very least, an averagely good shopping centre – and it has held this reputation for a century or more.

Obviously, there are considerable differences between the local shopping scene of 1895 and that of 1995 – not least in the relatively recent introduction of supermarkets and shopping precincts – yet, transported back one hundred

2. Shops once occupied the lower ground of Church Hill, seen here some time after the building of Harrow School's War Memorial buildings. The school house, Druries, was then reached through an archway on the left.

years, we would undoubtedly find a greater variety of shops than we might have expected.

The major difference would surely be one of location. Whereas virtually every part of our district now has its own substantial shopping parades, retailers in the last century were very largely concentrated on the top of Harrow Hill.

In this context, a glance at the Town Guide for 1850 is particularly instructive. Not only does it divide the town's citizens into 'gentry' and 'traders', it also lists no fewer than one hundred names in the latter category. As one would expect, there are many businesses essential to a horse-drawn age, among them saddle and harness-makers, wheelwrights and blacksmiths. There are others like tuck-shop keepers and straw hat makers that undoubtedly spring from the presence of Harrow School. The Guide even has the occasional entry that would surely have been unique at any time.

3. More shops were also found in the roads, such as West Street, that radiated off the Hill.

4. Shops first began to appear in the otherwise residential Station Road, Harrow, early this century. Among the first was Lidstones, the butchers, at the corner with St. Ann's Road.

5. Shoppers pass the St. Ann's Road brewery stores of Watney, Combe, Reid, one of an enormous variety of commercial ventures that made the street one of the busiest in the town.

Edward Goshawk, for example, is listed as both "bird stuffer and hair cutter".

The rest, however, are very much what we would expect to find serving any sizeable community today - three bakers, three butchers, a fishmonger, several grocers and greengrocers, a couple each of drapers, ironmongers and confectioners and at least six boot and shoe makers.

In common with the services and institutions of which we write elsewhere, a great many of these businesses were ultimately obliged to move away in order to expand. Yet this down-the-hill progression was initially slow until, around the turn of the century, Station Road (previously Greenhill Lane), was linked at the railway bridge to Peterborough Road.

Among those who successfully made the Hill to Greenhill transition was John Wright Cooper, a name that needs little introduction to older residents. Wright Cooper first set up business on the Hill in 1891 as baker and tuck-shop keeper but his real success dates from March 1929. In this month, Lady Percy, wife of a past president of the National Chamber of Trade, set in motion a gigantic mixing machine to symbolise the opening of No. 1 Greenhill Parade, Station Road, as both a

6. *At the Hill end of Station Road early this century, many of the big retail companies - Home and Colonial, Boots, Sainsburys - were already well established although there was still greenery on the other side of the road.*

7. *Looking down on the junction of College Road and Station Road in 1937 when the domes of the Harrow Coliseum (bottom centre) looked across to Boots, Lyons Tea Shop and Sainsburys.*

baker's shop and as a suite of restaurants-cum-reception rooms.

For almost half a century the Gayton Rooms, as they were called, catered for every conceivable kind of social, business and cultural activity in much the same way that the King's Head Hotel had served the community for most of the previous century. The Gayton Rooms even had its own Masonic Temple which at one time played host to some 50 different Masonic Lodges.

In the company's heyday, with other branches in Eastcote and Ruislip, there were some 160 employees on the permanent payroll.

Largely as a result of death duties – and to the widespread regret of the town – the Gayton Rooms were finally demolished in 1969. Ironically, they made way for a business, Universal Stationers, which was to enjoy, by comparison, only the briefest of life-spans.

Other early arrivals in Station Road were the

8. Another 1937 aerial shot showing Station Road near the junction with Bonnersfield Lane, following completion of the parade of shops known as Manor Parade after the old Manor House, still to be seen on the open ground behind. The framework of the Granada (now Cannon) Cinema, then under construction, can be seen at top right.

9. During World War I, Kenmare House in Station Road made way for Harrow's first department store, Sopers (later Debenhams). The store's subsequent enlargement swallowed up the adjoining public house, the Marquis of Granby.

10. *Both the College Road and Lowlands Road entrances to Harrow Metropolitan Station offered a number of lock-up shops, including Brentnall and Cleland, the coal merchants.*

brothers-in-law Thomas Lilley and William Skinner, who opened a boot warehouse on land they already owned at the corner with St. Ann's Road. From this ultimately grew the familiar chain of shoe shops that continues to bear their names.

Similarly, W.J. Soper is famed for giving his name to the department store - Harrow's first - with which he hoped to climax a long career as buyer for various West End drapery stores. As it proved, by the time his emporium finally opened on a handsome site opposite St. John's, Greenhill, World War I was in progress and business was initially slow; then, Soper fell victim to the influenza epidemic that followed the peace. Nevertheless, though the man was gone, his name and his store lived on. In the between-war years, it achieved such success that a major extension was required in 1937, which gave Harrow's shoppers over 100 different departments spread over some three acres of floor space.

Exactly 30 years later, there was a further substantial extension which, in the process, swallowed up the Marquis of Granby, the long established public house on the adjoining site.

11. Cullens, the grocers, were strongly represented in Harrow for much of the century. This was their West Harrow branch at the junction of Oxford Road and Pinner Road, as seen on an Edwardian postcard.

12. R. Smith Jnr. outside his family's riding boot business in Peterborough Road. The Smiths are said to have tended the young Winston Churchill when he fell from his cycle coming down the steep Peterborough Hill.

13. In the 1920s, Hubert Rigden ran The Greenhill Pharmacy at the corner of Peterborough Road and Grove Hill Road.

Only then, however, was the store name changed from Sopers to Debenhams although Green and Edwards, who had bought the company on Soper's death, had actually been a Debenham's subsidiary since the 1920s.

Sopers had always been something of a local landmark and, in truth, for several decades of this century, roads such as College Road and Station Road were largely defined by the shops they held. College Road then began with a cluster of shops around Roxborough Bridge, including the musty, dusty Sheppard's Book Shop, a haunt of true bibliophiles. Half-way along, before Harrow acquired a sizeable bus station, there were shops and business premises on both sides of the road, among them Capel's, the opticians; Clarke & Co, the estate agents; and backing on to the railway line, Webbs, the popular florist and landscape gardeners. The station forecourt, too, had a miscellany of small lock-up shops, among them Hinchcliffe's, the coal merchants.

14. College Road as it looked in the 1950s before the original Baptist Church with its distinctive tower had been rebuilt.

15. Even as late as 1973, College Road, near the Metropolitan station, still had a mix of shops, small businesses and residences in place of today's office blocks.

16. Northolt Road, looking towards Roxeth Corner, as many still remember it. All the little shops and cottages on the right have now given way to housing developments.

Virtually opposite the station entrance was the spacious building of the Grange Furnishing Stores with, just a few doors away, the smallest of the local Somertons, built to a highly individual design complete with fountained courtyard. In the 1930s Somertons, regarded as one of the town's more exclusive dress shops, also had substantial premises at the junction with Clarendon Road and in Station Road.

Though its two entertainment palaces – the Coliseum at one end and the Dominion at the other – were perhaps Station Road's most dominant buildings, this was always the road in which to seek the local branches of the big-name retailers. Sainsburys, whose splendid old-style grocer's shop only closed in September 1969, Boots, to which a lending library was later added, the Home and Colonial Stores and Freeman, Hardy and Willis were all well established there by the beginning of World War I.

17. Mr A.J. Abbott poses in the doorway of his cobbler's shop in Northolt Road. His companion is Jim Lambert, a former Barnardo's boy who became his apprentice.

18. Same man, same pose – different shop! Some years later, Jim Lambert was able to pose in front of his own cobbler's business some distance from the Harrow premises where he had learned his trade.

19. Pre-World War I, the Stiles family used to tour the district with a travelling version of their shop, situated opposite Roxeth gasworks in Northolt Road.

Other well remembered Station Road establishments of the 1930s and 1940s were, on one side, the Harrow Observer office and printing works with The Havelock Arms next door; and, on the other, the tiny Broadway Cinema and Broadway Lending Library; Nanette's, the shop for "smart gowns and knitwear and distinctive millinery"; the grocers, Harvey & Shillingford; Leonard Cave, the sports outfitters; and Felton's, the music store. Here, before making a purchase, shoppers were encouraged to play their choice of gramophone records in one of a number of individual music booths.

One day a whole book could - and possibly should - be written about the local shopping scene, for almost every part of the Borough can tell fascinating stories about its early shops and shop-keepers. Roxeth, for example, had the true forerunner to Sopers/Debenhams in Sladdens, the turn-of-the-century drapers and outfitters which occupied several adjoining

20. Even 80 or more years ago, newsagents, such as this little shop in Masons Avenue, Wealdstone, displayed the latest newspaper headlines, among them The People's promise of "Fulham Scandal - a girl's degradation".

21. The shop on the right with four hanging lanterns is Freeman, Hardy and Willis, one of a number of famous retailers - including Sainsburys, Cullens and the Home and Colonial, who had established themselves in Wealdstone High Street prior to 1914.

22. (left) Barnard's corner menswear shop at the junction of Wealdstone High Street as it looked in 1929.
23. (right) By 1958 the Barnards had added a storey to their premises topped by a sign proudly identifying the area as Barnard's Corner.

shop premises near the Timber Carriage public house at Roxeth Corner. As was so often the case, Sladdens was essentially a family business and Mr & Mrs Sladden made their home on the premises.

Similarly, today's corner shop MacDonalds in Wealdstone High Street was once a notable men's outfitters founded by the late W.J. Barnard and known as Barnard's Corner. Opened in 1904, Barnard's was rebuilt in 1929 and enlarged still further in 1959 until its advertisements could proudly claim "now four times its original size". But, in more recent times, the brothers Wreford and Frank Barnard found it increasingly difficult to compete with the big-name businesses.

In the 1980s, they went the way of so many excellent small retailers. Yet, if they remain largely unsung, there are still countless local homes in which such stores are still remembered with both gratitude and affection.

24. Hedges' sweet shop on the right attracts the small girls in this glimpse of the Marsh Road end of Bridge Street, Pinner, c.1900. Steam can be seen rising from the railway.

25. Chapel Lane, Pinner, around the turn of the century, looking towards the railway bridge and embankment. On the right is Jaques, the stationers and newsagents.

26. Pinner High Street in the year 1908, a picture almost certainly taken by Mrs Mary Emery who, for many years, ran The Bazaar (the shop on the right) which specialised in photographic materials.

27. In another pre-World War I picture, Fred Gurney appears with his family and staff outside his two well-stocked shops at 36-38 High Street, Pinner.

28. Delivery men stop for a chat in the snow outside Pinner Church c.1925. The larger vehicle came from Sainsburys, well-established in "Greenhill, Harrow" and other parts of the district.

29. In an era when food hygiene went largely uncontrolled, most butchers shops offered the kind of road-side display seen here c.1890 at A.S. Ginger's at the bottom of Stanmore Hill.

30. Around the turn of the century C.J. Gueran at the corner of Ealing Road and Burns Road, Sudbury, exemplified the well patronised "corner shop". They dealt in stationery, tobacco and "first class confectionery".

31. Many local traders and craftsmen operated from their own homes, such as H. Horrex who ran a boot and shoemaker's business from a cottage in Weald Place, College Road, Harrow Weald.

32. This undated, but possibly 1930s shot, shows the Sainsburys branch at 483 Kingsbury Road. Its frontage was typical of the stores opening throughout the area.

33. The delivery fleet of J. Brazier outside their Kenton Park Avenue dairy. As the window promised, all milk came from "our own cows at Kenton Grove Farm".

A Great Night Out

1. Before the advent of the cinema, less sophisticated - and more cruel - entertainment was offered by Italians who toured local streets (here Station Road, Wealdstone) with a performing bear.

Denigrators of today's 'on-tap' entertainment invariably point to the incomparable richness of the home-made amusements beloved of the Victorians and Edwardians. Yet the fact remains that, once an inexpensive mass-produced alternative was available - in the guise of moving pictures - people were remarkably quick to enjoy its pleasures.

This was certainly true in Harrow where travelling showmen - the first exhibitors - were

2. Opened in 1910, Central Harrow's first cinema was the Picturedrome adjoining the Royal Oak public house at the bottom of Clarendon Road.

drawing considerable audiences within a few years of the turn of the century.

Since film exhibition required no licence prior to 1910, these showmen could set up in any convenient local hall – or, for that matter, any decent-sized tent – thus making it virtually impossible to establish the precise location of Harrow's very first picture show.

The likeliest candidates are the so-called Star Theatre in Byron Road which was offering "the best that can be had from Pathe Freres" as early as 1909 and the more grandiose-sounding Rowley's Coliseum and Picture House in Masons Avenue. Significantly, both these operations were in Wealdstone, whose recently opened factories were able to furnish a ready-made audience eager for an hour or so's escapism.

What we now call Central Harrow had to wait a further year for "Living Pictures": then, two picture houses opened within the space of six months. First was the Harrow Picturedrome, apparently a conversion from 3 shops, in a large red-brick block at the end of Clarendon Road which older generations will

3. With remarkably few alterations to its facade, the Picturedrome was later converted into Adams Furnishing Stores. Trading continued in this building until the early 1980s.

4. From 1911 Wealdstone could boast a genuine "picture palace" in the Coronet, on the corner of High Street and Graham Road.

5. "Ten Nights In A Bar Room" was the principal attraction when the Coronet, ablaze with lights, was photographed one night c.1914.

6. Albert Brooks, popular manager of the Coronet, takes to the streets, thinly disguised, to promote his cinema's latest film, "A Sheik in Araby".

remember as Adams, the furniture stores.

"Such a place was sadly needed in the town" wrote the Harrow Observer, adding its hope that residents of places as far afield as Pinner and Ruislip would be attracted by "a cheap but high-class up-to-the-minute entertainment".

These hopes may not have been realised for the Picturedrome was obliged to close its doors after some three years; indeed, by March 1913, its proprietor was explaining to a bankruptcy examination that, whilst his weekly expenses averaged £40, his takings had never risen above £23.

At this time, most of the venues interspersed their short films with live variety acts. The Picturedrome gave prominent billing to a certain comedian called Mr. Wal E. Patch, almost certainly the entertainer who, as Wally Patch, became a regular and accomplished performer in British films of the 1930s and 40s.

Our next local cinema was the Harrow Cinema Theatre, better known by its later name of the Broadway. Operated by the Tipping family, the Broadway was built back from a parade of shops in Station Road, the original shop being transformed into an arcaded entrance behind which there was a tea

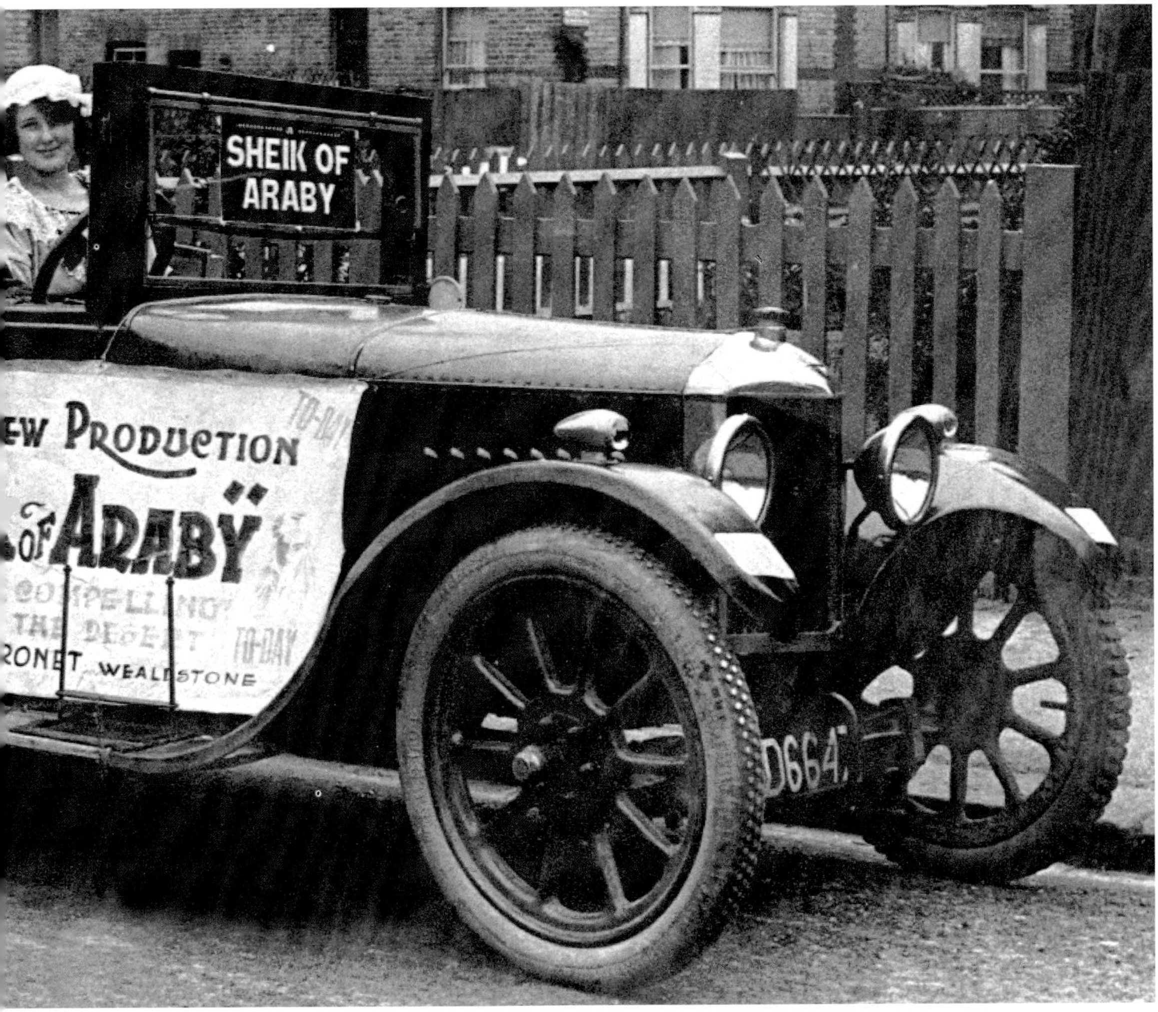

7. A close-up view of the handsome Coliseum in Station Road, Harrow, during its early years as a cinema. As the current attraction is Marlene Dietrich's "Blonde Venus", the date is around 1933.

8. Around 1921 the Coliseum could still boast an impressive forecourt although this was later diminished by road-widening and the building of shops on either side.

lounge and a 400-seater cinema. Thanks in part to the hundreds of young people attending the Harrow Technical College right next door, the Broadway managed to survive until the start of World War II.

Not to be outdone, Wealdstone then opened a new attraction called the Bioscope at the High Street junction with Graham Road. Shortly after the opening, its proprietor, Florence Hall, was sued by her architect for an outstanding debt of £25; nevertheless, the venture proved highly successful and that December, a large local press advertisement advised patrons that the hall was now comfortably heated. Later, the premises were briefly known as the Wealdstone Cinema although its greatest success was achieved under the name of the Coronet.

From 1918 to 1936, the Coronet was managed by a Wolseley Road resident called Albert Brooks who, interviewed during his retirement, recalled with special affection the Coronet's little curtained boxes at the back. These, he not surprisingly claimed, were "habitually occupied by courting couples".

When the Coronet was eventually pulled down in the late 1930s, a new cinema rapidly

9. The Harrow Coliseum, as many still remember it, flanked by shops in a totally built-up Station Road. Its site now houses an Iceland Supermarket.

10. The Embassy in North Harrow was opened by British film star Betty Balfour in October 1929. It, too, has since given way to a supermarket.

11. Situated at the top of Bridge Street, Pinner's only cinema opened as the Langham in 1936. It had become the ABC Cinema when this picture was taken in 1947.

rose on the site. This was the well-remembered Herga, which survived until 1951, and was almost certainly the first cinema in the district to experiment with the occasional sub-titled European film alongside its more usual fare of double bills of older films, changed twice weekly.

Like the Bioscope-cum-Coronet many other local cinemas changed their names with a frequency that makes it difficult to chart their careers. Sometimes, the new name reflected a refurbishment but, more generally, a more grandiose name was simply an attempt to convince patrons that the cinema concerned had travelled a long way from its fairground origins.

An exception was the one and only cinema on Harrow Hill which actually reversed this trend, going from the Elite, the name under which it was launched in 1920, to the Cosy.

Older residents will confirm that the latter was certainly the more appropriate name for an essentially modest hall – in fact, the name came top of a patron poll to rechristen the cinema on its renovation in the early 1930s. Later, for reasons that are now unclear, this building opposite the King's Head Hotel (and once the town's public hall) became the Carlton. The locals naturally continued to call it the Cosy although, in truth, its days were already numbered. In August 1939, the lessee stood in the dock at Wealdstone Petty Sessions accused of having obtained credit whilst an undischarged bankrupt. Among those pressing payment for films supplied were Exclusive Films, Butchers Films and the newsreel

12. Although no longer used as a cinema, this unique art deco architecture has ensured the survival of the former Grosvenor, Rayners Lane, here photographed during its years as an Odeon.

13. Wembley High Road also had its share of now-vanished cinemas. This is the Odeon as it looked towards the end of its life in 1960.

company, Pathe.

By the late thirties, of course, these relatively small independent cinemas were all beginning to feel the impact of the much grander cinemas now springing up all over the district. These included Harrow's two great surviving cinemas – the former Cannon in Station Road (opened as the Dominion in January 1936) and the Cannon in Sheepcote Road (which, as the Granada, was opened in October 1937 by movie star and subsequent local resident Jessie Matthews).

As originally built, both cinemas were truly picture palaces, the original Dominion holding 2,500 and the Granada accommodating 2,222 in settings of considerable luxury.

It is often forgotten that the Dominion was designed by the same F.E. Bromige who was responsible later that year for the more famous Grosvenor in Rayners Lane. As built, the Dominion had an almost futuristic facade featuring seemingly acres of curved glass. Subsequently – and sadly – this fell victim to an "improvement" scheme which concealed its glories behind the still-extant but highly anonymous blue cladding. At the time of writing, this familiar building has begun a new chapter in its life with a new name (The Safari) and a new policy – the showing of exclusively Asian films.

The Odeon circuit opened its first-ever North-West London cinema in South Harrow in 1933 and, following its success, they were quick to develop other imposing sites for Odeons in Kenton, Wealdstone, Sudbury and Kingsbury.

Unfortunately, the great cinema-going years of the 1930s and 40s (when a night at the pictures was a genuine morale booster) were not to be maintained and, with one exception, virtually every trace of the distinctive Odeon-style architecture had vanished from the district by the early 1970s.

The exception is the aforementioned Grosvenor at Rayners Lane. Though its name

14. No reference to local entertainment would be complete without the inclusion of Pinner Fair, which was founded by Royal Charter in 1336. It was thus well over 500 years old when this rare picture was taken around the turn of the century.

15. Crowds were already beginning to build up in Bridge Street, Pinner, when this picture was taken on a typical Fair day in the early 1920s.

was frequently altered – at various times, it was an Odeon, a Gaumont and an Ace – its design remained unchanged. Today, with its curving concrete facade, often likened to a stylised elephant's trunk, it is a very special example of mid-thirties Cinema Art Deco, and has been saved from demolition by the award of a Grade II listing for architectural merit. Nobody, however, has managed to perpetuate its use as a cinema although, at the time of writing, it has reverted to its original name of Grosvenor and its former cafe is in use as "an unique cine-bar experience".

The ABC circuit was also strongly represented in the area, the Embassy in North Harrow having been opened as early as October 1929. It was actually built on ground made more than a little marshy by a nearby stream and suffered subsidence problems in subsequent years. In 1936 these even forced its temporary closure when the balcony cracked with an audible report and the audience had to be evacuated. The same circuit also opened, within days of the launch of the Dominion, the sizeable Langham Cinema at the top of Bridge Street, Pinner.

Warmly as many of these cinemas are remembered, the place of entertainment that still seems to evoke the fondest local memories is the long-lost legitimate theatre, the Harrow Coliseum. With its important site in Station Road (where the Iceland Superstore stands today) and its impressive design dominated by two open-sided cupolas, it was so much a part of the local scene that many people still find it hard to believe that it vanished forever as long ago as 1958.

The Coliseum, too, was actually built as a 2,000-seater cinema. The first press announcements in 1919 even called it the "Electric Coliseum", but in May 1940, Sir Alfred Denville, a great man of the theatre, re-opened it as the town's first – and, as it

16. *Pinner Fair as it looked to a cameraman on the roof of Pinner Parish Church in 1930. Many of the showmen returned year after year, including the Pettigroves who ran the popular carousel for more than a century.*

It was always rumoured that Denville salvaged the curtain and many of the furnishings from London's famous Gaiety Theatre: certainly, the theatre historian W MacQueen Pope recalls Denville buying three rows of Gaiety stalls for the equivalent of £3.75.

In its new form, the Coliseum played host to every conceivable kind of production, featuring stars as diverse as the Shakespearean Donald Wolfit, the renowned tenor, Richard Tauber, the well-remembered Carl Rosa Opera Company, even Nellie Wallace, one of the surviving greats of the music hall era. And, of course, there was always a pantomime at Christmas.

Wartime houses were generally large and enthusiastic but, in the next decade, the theatre began to suffer from the competition of TV and the fact that the whole range of West End theatre was only some 40 minutes away by Tube.

Ironically, it was Denville himself who was largely responsible for the theatre's ultimate closure. When he died at his South Hill Avenue home in March 1955, his will directed that the Coliseum be sold "as soon as may be convenient". At a six-hour public enquiry, it was revealed that the theatre impresario, Alfred Esdaile, was willing to pay £49,000 to maintain it as a theatre - this, remember, was a full 40 years ago. The largest offers, however, were all from multiple stores with Express Supermarkets making by far the highest bid at £67,000.

Despite considerable local agitation, the demolition men finally arrived in September 1958. They quickly razed to the ground a unique local asset, only to replace it with one more example of an undertaking not exactly in short supply.

No Half Measures

1. A rare photograph of the old Crown and Anchor beside the gates of Harrow School. This picture was taken some time after 1863 from the garden of the newly built Vaughan Library.

"Drink is the curse of this place", wrote the Vicar of Wembley around 1873.

John Cunningham, Vicar of Harrow (1811-1861) had said much the same thing some 40 years before when giving evidence before a Select Commission for the Observance of the Sabbath Day. Although Cunningham's main complaints were levelled against local farmers who often failed to pay their men until Sunday morning, he also levelled some criticism at the men themselves for immediately taking themselves off to the shops or, more likely, the beer houses.

In one respect, at least, it is easy to have some sympathy with the beer-drinking men. For the first half of the last century, drinking water was often both scarce and costly in Harrow. Beer, on the other hand, was readily available - and cheap.

2. Around the turn of the century, coaches and horses were a familiar sight at The King's Head, Harrow Hill, which maintained its own stables.

Though it was obviously intended to provide a measure of control over the sale of liquor, especially spirits, the Duke of Wellington's Beerhouse Act in 1830 allowed any householder assessed on the Poor Rate to retail beer at his or her domestic premises. Admittedly, they had to pay the not inconsiderable sum of two guineas (just over £2) for the privilege, but the resulting trade seems to have been remarkably free from restriction (although they were forbidden to open before four in the morning!)

The inevitable result was a rapid proliferation of drinking places; indeed, by 1873, Harrow could lay claim to 27 inns and 27 beerhouses, which worked out at one drinking place for every 157 of the population.

Many of them were established in what we would now regard as highly unlikely situations – the well regarded Crown and Anchor, for example, was built right next door to the main gates of the principal Harrow School building, the so-called Old Schools. It was also only a few yards from the parish church of St. Mary's, although this appears to have been

3. There is still a White Horse in Middle Road, although a very different building from this Edwardian original, one of many local inns managed by the Farmborough family.

4. Although the timbered facade of the Kingsfield Arms still looks much the same today, its setting in Bessborough Road has changed almost beyond recognition.

5. Here, photographed in the 1920s, The Cricketers at the junction of West Street and Nelson Road, Harrow Hill, is now a private house.

much to the liking of the parish who regularly used the inn as a venue for their Vestry Meetings.

Harrow School boys (regularly served so-called 'small' beer as part of their school diet) also found its presence useful – indeed, during the years its licence was held by a certain John Bliss, it was known affectionately to the boys as "The abode of bliss".

In the 1860s, however, the School Governors found it convenient to buy the property as a residence for the School Custos, whereupon the licensed business moved to a house at the top of West Street.

At the opposite end of the Hill's High Street was the no less famous establishment called "The King's Head". Possibly because the name commemorates King Henry VIII, tradition has

6. When demolished in 1961, the little Three Horseshoes and its adjoining pond in Northolt Road, South Harrow, had been a feature of local life for well over 200 years.

7. A rare picture of the first Half Moon at Roxeth Corner originally created through the conversion of two cottages at the foot of Roxeth Hill. In 1862, it was licensed to Abraham Farmborough.

8. The present Half Moon shortly after its opening in 1893. Sladdons, the drapers, on the other corner was Harrow's biggest store until Sopers (Debenhams) was built.

it that the building was once the monarch's hunting lodge; indeed, for much of this century, the year 1536 was inscribed on the inn's facade. Yet there are no surviving records to support this claim and its first recorded appearance in print is in a Harrow Vestry Minute of August 1706.

'The King's Head' achieved its peak of fame during Victorian times when, prior to the building of a Public Hall, it was the centre of virtually every social and political activity in the town. In more recent times it has lost its licence, although the building itself is still in use as a social services hostel.

At the end of the 19th century, the Hill could also lay claim to The White Hart, The Castle, The White Horse and, at the very bottom, The Half Moon (all of which remain), together with The Cricketers in West Street, the little Lord Nelson in Nelson Road and The North Star, The Crown and The Bricklayers Arms, all in Crown Street. As late as 1907, in fact, the police opposed the relicensing of the latter on the grounds that there were then nine licensed houses and four off-licences within a quarter of a mile.

The community of shops, houses and factories that had grown up around the first Harrow and Wealdstone station was hardly less well served with drinking places. Like their Hill

9. Originally 18th century but rebuilt in 1925, The Marquis of Granby was finally lost when the former Sopers department store extended its frontage on Station Road.

10. Now the oldest building in the vicinity of the St Ann's Centre, the Royal Oak was built c.1900 on the site of an earlier beerhouse.

11. The rarely seen Rose and Crown in Kenton Lane, near the still-surviving 'Duck In The Pond'. Rose Farm flats now occupy this site.

counterparts, most adopted either highly traditional names or specifically local ones. The Cricketers, for example, was within batting distance of Harrow School's cricket pitch.

But what are we to make of that most curious name, "The Case Is Altered", of which two examples remain in the Borough - one in Wealdstone's High Street, the other picturesquely set at Old Redding. In neither case does there appear to be any genuinely authenticated local explanation although, for years, a nice little story was advanced on behalf of the Wealdstone premises. This was inspired by the building of the London-Birmingham railway through Wealdstone in the 1830s which, as we've seen elsewhere, brought scores of hard-drinking navvies to the district. It seems that a kind-hearted landlady originally allowed them to drink on credit until the inevitable day she was replaced by a rule-abiding termagant. In the face of frequent reminders of her predecessor's generosity, this lady was said to have used but

12. The original Rest Hotel at Kenton, seven years after its 1900 opening when its well-appointed rooms and 18 acres of grounds attracted something of an upmarket clientele.

13. An undated photograph of The Rest Hotel when it played host to a meeting of the Hunt.

14. An early picture (c.1885) of The Queen's Head in High Street, Pinner, when it still had a front garden enclosed by a timber fence.

one response – "the case is altered".

Other, more overtly historical explanations can be found, including the suggestion that the name is really The Cause Is Altered, a reference to former Royalist houses that switched sides once Cromwell had won the Civil War.

Yet another theory looks back even further to the distinguished Catholic lawyer Edmund Plowden (1518-1585) who was once tricked by an agent provocateur garbed as a priest into attending a false Mass. At his trial, having discovered the true identity of his betrayer, Plowden firmly declared "No priest. No mass. The case is altered". This reputedly became a popular catchphrase and certainly can be found in the writings of Ben Johnson and his contemporaries.

Our local hostelries, however, seem to prefer what might be termed the "Spanish versions". Although the Wealdstone house now has a sign without any illustration, there was a time when it boasted a picture of Spanish dancers, presumably in acknowledgement of the "casa del saltar" theory. This argued that soldiers returning from the Peninsular War wished to

15. Customers gather outside The Queen's Head, Pinner towards the end of the last century to admire a notably picturesque coster's cart.

16. A popular alternative to the Pinner public houses in 1895 was The Cocoa Tree Coffee Tavern (with flag pole), a private house rebuilt as a temperance tavern with extensive pleasure gardens.

17. Horse and dray belonging to Clutterbucks, the Stanmore Hill brewery, take voters to the polls for a 1906 local election.

be reminded of the dance halls in which they had spent happy off-duty hours although, in truth, the Spanish verb 'saltar' refers not to social dancing but to jumping with joy – or pain!

By contrast, the Old Redding pub, unhesitatingly plumps for the alternative 'Spanish' explanation. Both its sign and an explanatory bar plaque clearly relate the present name to 'Casa Alta', a house or inn on high ground patronised by the self-same British soldiers during the Peninsular War. Given that many local men belonged to the 57th Regiment of Foot (later the Middlesex Regiment) and that the Old Redding house is just old enough to have been opened by a Peninsular veteran, the writer inclines towards this version.

At the same time, he admits that the theory might go down even better after a drink or two – ideally at the local hostelry

18. A more recent picture of the former Clutterbucks Brewery, now partially redeveloped as apartments. From 1763 until 1923, the brewery was run by successive generations of Clutterbucks.

19. A 1930s photograph of The Abercorn Arms on Stanmore Hill, famously visited by the Prince Regent in 1814.

20. When horse-drawn traffic ruled the roads, this was Wealdstone's The Case is Altered. Note the highly unusual wicker chaise on the right.

21. Harrow's other Case Is Altered, photographed between the World Wars when the still picturesque Old Redding was even more rural.

22. The first Red Lion in Harrow Weald stands to the right of this very peaceful picture of College Road, named after the long-vanished St. Andrew's College.

23. *(right) The Red Lion's ostler in 1905.*

24. *(below) A mounted troop rides into the forecourt of the original Ballot Box on Horsenden Hill in this highly evocative picture dating from 1914.*

Giving Praise

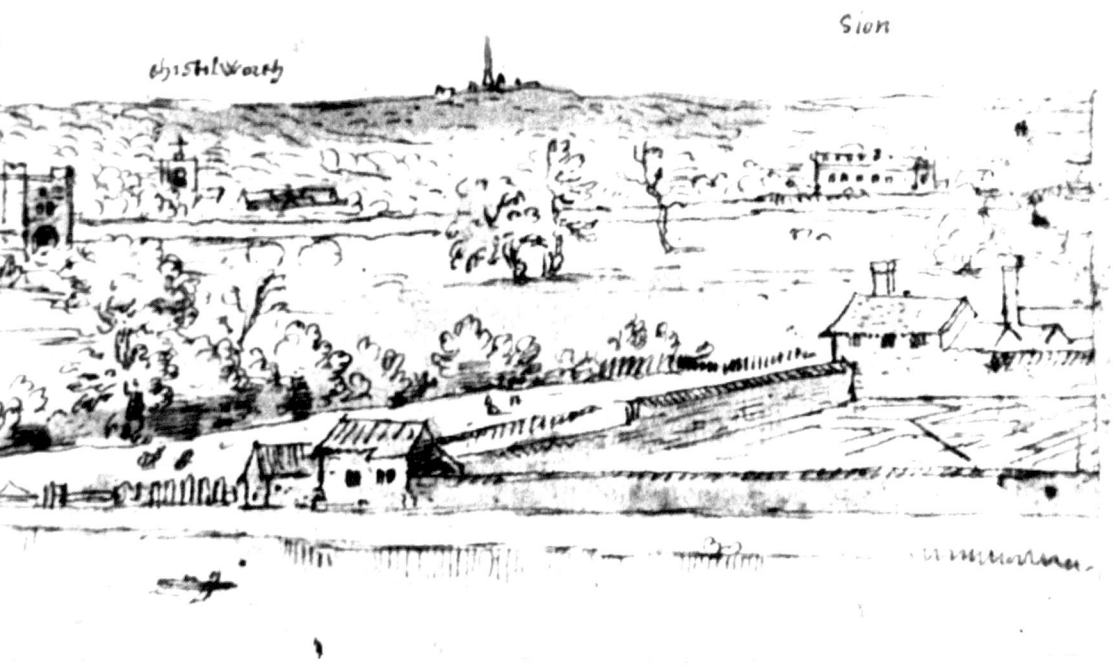

1. Dating from 1562, the earliest known drawing of St. Mary's Harrow On The Hill (identified as Haravil), shows the spire rising from the Middlesex landscape between Isleworth Church and Syon House.

In this increasingly secular age it may be difficult for us to envision a time when one institution – and one alone – was at the heart of every aspect of local life. This was, of course, the church. And for centuries 'the church' meant St. Mary's, Harrow On The Hill, founded as long ago as 1087.

There may even have been an earlier church on the same commanding site, for William the Conqueror's Domesday Book of 1068 records the presence of a priest on Harrow

2. From a distance the exterior of St. Mary's in 1838 looks much like the church today. A closer look, however, reveals rough cast walls, an unbattlemented roof and a tower with both clock and sundial.

Hill with a considerable holding of land. There is no mention of an actual church but, since Domesday was more concerned with land than with buildings, any existing church may not have been considered important enough to record.

There is also a Domesday record of a priest at Great Stanmore although, again, it is without any reference to a Stanmore Church: nevertheless documentary evidence does exist for some kind of Stanmore church building from the start of the 12th century.

The Manor of Little Stanmore (recorded as Stanmer in Domesday Book), also appears to have had a church of St. Lawrence as early as the 12th century although the earliest part of the present St. Lawrence, Whitchurch, is its early 16th century tower.

No records survive of other early churches in the vicinity although we know that, in medieval times, a number of independent chantry chapels were in use locally. In addition, where Bentley Priory stands today, there was,

3. With its characteristic Norman zig-zag decoration, the lintel above St. Mary's West Door is the oldest visible reminder of the church's 900 year history.

4. Removed from the South porch to its present Northern position during Gilbert Scott's restoration, this ancient nail studded door remains one of the treasures of St. Mary's.

5. In close-up, St. Mary's nave roof reveals a wealth of detailed carving barely visible from the body of the church, including a series of angels each carrying a different medieval musical instrument.

for a time, an Augustinian house dependent upon the priory of St. Gregory, Canterbury.

Any narrative about our early church-going therefore returns again and again to St. Mary's, whose parish boundaries once encompassed most of today's Harrow Borough (Stanmore apart) as well as a great deal of the neighbouring Borough of Brent.

In its early days, St. Mary's also had a national as opposed to a local significance in that from AD 825, for seven full centuries, successive Archbishops of Canterbury were also Lords of the Manor of Harrow. Over the years this gave St. Mary's a roll-call of famous celebrants that few other parish churches could match, and there is ample proof that the early Archbishops took a genuine personal interest in the Church on The Hill.

Archbishop Anselm (later canonized as St. Anselm) personally performed the consecration ceremony in 1094 and there are at least three

6. *One of the first Governors of Harrow School, William Gerrard, is seen with a lady traditionally identified as his sister in this fine alabaster effigy in the North Transept of St. Mary's.*

7. In this Ackermann lithograph of 1816 we see St. Mary's some 30 years before its mid-19th century restoration. Note the heavy box pews and the old reredos bearing the Ten Commandments.

authoritative records of visits by Archbishop Thomas Becket, one just a few days before his murder at Canterbury Cathedral.

It would be fascinating to think that today's parish church is essentially the building that Becket knew but, inevitably, St. Mary's is an intriguing amalgam of work done over many centuries in many styles (although given some degree of unity by the restoration activities of Gilbert Scott in the mid 1840s).

The West Door, with its Norman zig-zag ornamentation, remains the oldest part. The spire, added by Rector John Byrkhede around 1451, remains its most famous feature. It was, of course, the sight of the spire, clearly in view from his Royal Palace, that prompted King Charles II to describe St. Mary's as "The Most Visible Church", a description hardly less accurate today and one of which the parish is justifiably proud.

Pinner's beautiful old church of St. John (dedicated in 1321 on the site of an even earlier chapel) was, from its earliest days, part of the parish of St. Mary's, only achieving full parochial independence in 1766.

Greater Stanmore's church, on the other hand, was always wholly independent. The first church, however, was considered too far from the village centre and, in July 1632, a new edifice was consecrated by William Laud, then Bishop of London. The fact that all the expenses of building had been borne by Sir John Wolstenholme was later used against Laud (by now, Archbishop of Canterbury) by the Puritans who claimed that "he outwent Popery in the consecration of chapels". In this instance, at least, Laud was rightly able to claim that this was no private chapel but a true parish church.

During the next century it would seem that only patchwork was required to keep our churches in good order, but the steady growth of population in the 1800s, especially after the railway's arrival, saw the fabric of St. Mary's stretched to the very seams.

8. Apart from the Harrow boys' gallery on the left and the subsequently replaced East window, St. Mary's after its restoration looked much the same as it does today.

St. Mary's, admittedly, had a highly specific problem of accommodation. In accordance with the written instructions of John Lyon, founder of Harrow School, Harrow boys had always worshipped in the parish church, largely occupying the special galleries created for them.

By the mid-1830s, however, there was a strong feeling that local residents were actually being excluded because of the sheer number of boys. There was also resentment that, whereas virtually anyone with means paid for their pews, the boys could worship free-of-charge! Furthermore, the boys were frequently restive during sermons whose subject matter and length often went well beyond the limits of their intellect and endurance.

Not surprisingly, the Governors were prompted to lay plans for creating a chapel of their very own but this entirely sensible idea was vigorously resisted by the-then Vicar of Harrow, the redoubtable John Cunningham, himself a School Governor; indeed, even after the consecration of a modest School Chapel in 1837, the School bowed to Cunningham's views by allowing the boys to attend Matins at St. Mary's. Evensong, however, was held in the Chapel.

As it happened, the ultimate loss of the boys was more than compensated by the number of newcomers arriving in the district and, towards the end of his 50-year ministry, Cunningham was obliged to turn his time and talents to the provision of daughter churches.

The first to arise was All Saints at Harrow Weald, consecrated in 1850. Next, Anne and Frances Copland, having inherited Sudbury Lodge and its estate, not only gave the land for a church but also met the cost of its building (again to a design by Gilbert Scott). This was St. John the Evangelist, Wembley, intended to serve the-then hamlets of Wembley, Alperton and Preston as well as part of Sudbury.

Christ Church, Roxeth Hill, followed in 1862, the year after Cunningham's death, to designs by the increasingly active Scott practice. Having been notably generous in the provision

9. Although St. Mary's Vicarage on Church Hill is largely Victorian there has been a Vicarage on this particular site for over 750 years.

10. Harrow's vicars have always lived in close proximity to Harrow School as this unusual garden view reveals. On the left is the Vicarage drawing room; on the right, the back of Old Schools.

of memorials to the old Vicar – among them the beautiful St. Mary's lych gate – the parish then discovered among his papers that Cunningham had cherished his own idea of a suitable memorial. This was a District Church down the hill in Greenhill.

Accordingly, in December 1866, a small if remarkably ornate brick church was consecrated in the name of St. John The Baptist on the corner of Station Road and Sheepcote Road. Of Italianate design, it was especially notable for the curiously conical roof of its (separate) bell-tower, earning it the local sobriquet of "the candle snuffer". This building, however, quickly proved too small for

11. In Edwardian times, as now, the famous lych-gate of St. Mary's was considered an ideal spot for family photographs.

12. In Sunday best, St. Mary's choir pose for a formal studio portrait in 1869.

13. With a symbolic bell rope on the ground before them, St. Mary's bell-ringers provide a reminder of how church folk dressed around 1905.

its fast growing neighbourhood and it was replaced by a new church that eventually grew into today's St. John's.

In all, some nine daughter churches of St. Mary's were built within the space of 80 years and this has been followed by the addition of a further eleven churches during the last half century.

By now, of course, the town could claim many alternatives to the so-called Established Church. As early as 1812, a Particular Baptist Church had opened in Byron Hill Road, prompting a nasty incident when a special boat bearing inaugural guests along the Paddington-Greenford Canal was pelted with mud and stones, possibly by Harrow boys and adherents of the Established Church.

Together with a well in its grounds for total immersion baptism, this chapel survived for some 50 years. It was then replaced by a new chapel on the same site in fashionable Victorian Gothic style. Still surviving, this handsome structure has since seen service as school classrooms, as the well-remembered Hill Laundry and, currently, as a wire-working factory.

14. *Pinner Church as it looked in 1807 when Walter Williams, once its curate, had become Vicar of Harrow.*

15. *The ruins of Stanmore Old Church consecrated in 1632 as they looked in 1906. The building still stands though the highly destructive ivy has long since been removed.*

16. The first of St. Mary's many daughter churches was All Saints, Harrow Weald, consecrated in 1850.

The Wesleyans, too, built themselves a chapel on Roxeth Hill before moving to what is now the Welsh chapel in Lower Road and later to a large custom-built chapel in Bessborough Road.

Those of the Roman faith had to wait rather longer for an established meeting place of their own. The very hint of such a building in 1855 provoked much unfriendly correspondence in the Harrow Gazette. Someone calling himself "Layman of the Church of England" even wrote that "such a prospect (should) stir up every Protestant... to see that it is through no neglect of his that any standing room is afforded to the encroachment of an alien faith".

Happily, local Catholics found a notable champion in the distinguished churchman, Cardinal Manning, who had entered Harrow School as a boy shortly after Vicar Cunningham had become a Governor. In 1878, Manning invited a group of Belgian nuns from the 3rd Order of St. Dominic's to Harrow where they took up residence on the site that subsequently became St. Dominic's Convent (later Grammar) School. Some years later, with Manning's continued support, Harrow Hill gained its first Catholic mission in Roxborough Park.

Here the little iron building slowly grew into today's fine church. Given Harrow's history, its name is especially appropriate – The Church of Our Lady and St. Thomas of Canterbury.

17. *An exceptionally rare picture of the first St. John's, Greenhill, which rose on the corner of Sheepcote Road and Station Road in 1866. Italianate in design, it had a separate bell tower (glimpsed through the trees) whose conical roof won it the nick-name "the candle snuffer".*

18. *The second St. John's and its adjoining parish hall, known as the Victoria Hall, immediately prior to World War I. Always a popular meeting place, Victoria Hall became a Government backed British Restaurant during World War II.*

19. *An early picture of Christ Church, Roxeth Hill, built around 1862 by Gilbert Scott who restored St. Mary's and gave Harrow School the Vaughan Library and Chapel buildings.*

20. *Bessborough Road Methodist Church photographed shortly after its opening in 1905. The last service before its demolition was held in May 1977.*

21. *College Road Baptist Church as it looked in 1978. Four years later it was demolished and a new church built as part of an ambitious multi-purpose development.*

22. When first opened early this century, St. Peter's, West Harrow, occupied one of the first-ever prefabricated structures. The later and grander church closed in the early 1980s, subsequently becoming a Christian Centre.

23. Wealdstone's first church was Holy Trinity at the High Street junction with Headstone Drive. Originally the nave was only three bays long, the extension nearest the camera being added in 1903.

24. The great Catholic churchman Cardinal Manning, himself an Old Harrovian, did much to establish Harrow's first Catholic mission in Roxborough Park, which became today's Church of Our Lady and St. Thomas of Canterbury.

Sporting Traditions

1. Harrow School boys practising archery on Church Fields - a late 18th century print from Lyson's guide book 'The Environs of London' and now in the Harrow Local History Collection.

Harrow's sporting traditions might be said to go back at least as far as the reign of the first Queen Elizabeth. It was then that John Lyon first wrote about games in his amazingly detailed rules for the conduct of the School for which his monarch had just granted a Royal Charter.

According to these rules, the scholars – the forerunners of today's Harrow schoolboys – "shall not be permitted to play, except upon Thursday only sometimes when the weather is fine, and upon Saturday or half-holidays or after evening prayer".

He was equally precise about the nature of this play, which he insisted should be "to drive

2. Once the Silver Arrow tournament was banned in 1771, cricket began to take over as the dominant game at Harrow School, as revealed in this 1772 portrait of young William and Jack Mason standing at a somewhat unusual wicket.

a top, to toss a handball, to run, or to shoot, and none other". By shooting, he meant, of course, the shooting of bows and arrows.

Inevitably, archery came to be the School's principal sporting activity and, in 1648, Sir Gilbert Talbot, a well-known local resident, presented the School with a specially-made Silver Arrow as the prize for an annual archery tournament.

So began a tradition which endured for some 123 years, the tournament quickly becoming as much a social as a sporting event with the contestants elaborately clad in silks and satins.

Even those boys among the spectators wanted to look their best for the occasion and the Harrow School Archives still hold a remarkably touching letter from the schoolboy Richard Brinsley Sheridan. Writing to his uncle, the playwright-to-be begs for a new suit of clothes especially for the tournament because, as he very candidly admits, his day-to-day clothes

3. Harrow School's 6th Form Cricket Ground still presents perhaps the least changed aspect of Harrow Hill, as this photograph from 1874 clearly shows.

4. All Saints, Harrow Weald, Football Club photographed at Harrow Weald Recreation Ground c.1905. The older gentleman is the Vicar, the Rev. W.H. Peers, a keen supporter and occasional referee.

5. In Victorian times, Harrow Weald also boasted a successful cricket eleven. This group picture was taken in 1896, the year Kodak staged its first all ladies' cricket match.

"having met with a few accidents", were hardly notable for their cleanliness.

Ultimately, the Silver Arrow became the victim of its own success. Each year, it seems, it assumed such importance in the school calendar that academic work was largely neglected. Each year, too, it drew bigger and less disciplined crowds. Finally in 1771, after a spectator had been hit in the face, the then Head Master Benjamin Heath decided to call a halt.

Perhaps more surprisingly, the record books reveal a close Harrovian link with a far more famous annual sporting event, the All England Lawn Tennis Championships at Wimbledon Spencer Gore, the very first name to be inscribed on the men's championship roll in 1877 was, in fact, an old boy of Bradbys, the Harrow School house in the High Street. When he lost his title the following year, it was to P.F. (Frank) Hadow whose family lived at Sudbury Priory.

John Hartley, champion of 1879 and 1880, was also an Old Harrovian. By vocation a parish priest, it is always said that during his first championship year he was obliged to rush home to Yorkshire to conduct the Sunday service!

Such Old Harrovian sporting victories must surely have been much talked-about in the

6. *Crowds on Roxborough Bridge cheer the first runner to reach Harrow during the 1908 Olympic Marathon.*

7. *The adult entry for the 1908 Harrow Marathon lines up for the start in Harrow Recreation Ground.*

8. Fired by Marathon fever, the Harrow Observer staged a purely local event in October 1908. The winner was Banks, who worked for a Station Road butcher.

close-knit School community and could well have inspired the two daughters of the Rev. A. W. Watson, a Harrow master, to improve their game. Certainly, when Wimbledon announced a women's championship in 1884, both girls not only entered but actually progressed to the final when Maud, the younger, defeated sister Lillian 6-8, 6-3, 6-3.

As the tennis historian Max Robertson has commented, there were no special rules or precedents for what women players should wear so the finalists turned out in much the same kind of long-sleeved, long-skirted dress they would have worn to a garden party. The only probable dress concession was a pair of flat shoes, possibly with India rubber soles.

Maud, incidentally, won the Wimbledon Championship again the following year and also picked up the Irish and Welsh tennis titles.

Local athletics received another remarkable boost in 1908 when the London-based Olympic Games chose a marathon route that began in Windsor and passed through Ruislip, Pinner and Harrow.

As shown in the photographs of the day, the first runner through Harrow was the South African Hefferson who, in the event, came second to J.J. Hayes of the United States (Pietro Dorandi of Italy was actually first into the stadium but, near exhaustion, he had been clutched by would-be helping hands that merely ensured his disqualification!)

Evidently, one of the most popular places to view the Marathon was the Pinner Road premises of the Leabourne Manufacturing Company - "repairers to the Royal Automobile Club" as their local press advertisements proudly proclaimed. With some ingenuity, they had made arrangements with the Press Association to supply a continuous report of the race and so were able to put up regular progress details on a large display board in the Pinner Road.

Such was the local interest in the Olympic Marathon that the local newspaper decided to organise its own marathon in the October of

9. Suddenly Marathons were all the rage - and the London Evening News sponsored another, won by Girot, pictured here in Lowlands Road outside the estate offices of E.A. Crooke & Co

10. Over 90 years ago Roxeth Corner, looking much as it does today, provides the background for the start of a special Roxeth Marathon.

the same year, beginning and ending in Harrow Recreation Ground in Pinner Road. There were three races though none of true marathon status. The men ran eleven and a quarter miles, the youths eight miles and the boys, some five miles.

With 59 runners, the men's race was particularly well contested, there being great rivalry between runners from Harrow and from Wealdstone. The latter, however, took all the honours, producing not only the winner but also seven out of the first twelve to finish.

The event was considered sufficiently successful to be repeated the following year although the now well-known Harrow Marathon did not become an annual event until more recent times.

In the 1930s, Harrow again had a special interest in the Wimbledon title when, for three years in succession, it was won by the great Fred Perry, a one-time Ealing County School pupil and a member of the local Herga Tennis Club.

In 1939, Jean Nicoll, a former pupil of St. Margaret's School in Station Road was said by the experts to be "as good as (Suzanne) Lenglen at her age". Unluckily for her, the outbreak of World War II put a temporary check to her ambitions and, when Wimbledon resumed, the (admittedly considerable) best she could achieve - now as Mrs Jean Bostock - was a Quarter Final place in 1946, 1947 and 1948.

Just six years later, the town had even greater cause for pride when a "son of Harrow" (as he was invariably dubbed) achieved a record that made him the focus of excited attention not just in Harrow but throughout the world. His name - and older readers will surely need little prompting -was Roger (now Sir Roger) Bannister who, at Iffley Road, Oxford, ran the world's first 4-minute mile.

Though his career has since taken him far from Harrow - from 1985 to 1993 he was Master of Pembroke College, Oxford - Roger Bannister was truly "a local lad". The son of

11. *Jean Nicholl (right) partners Pauline Betz in the 1946 Wightman Cup.*

Ralph and Alice Bannister, he lived first in Butler Road, later moving to 89 Whitmore Road. He then followed his sister Joyce to Vaughan Road Infants School, whose admission register is now fittingly lodged in the Harrow Local History Collection. It shows that the young Bannister arrived at the school in April 1937 and remained until November 1939.

In his book *First Four Minutes*, he writes of the value of fright as an aid to speed and recalls how hard he ran on hearing his first air-raid siren. (At the time, he was sailing his boat on a pond some half a mile from home!)

With typical generosity, Bannister offered the Amateur Athletics Association half the royalties from his book towards the creation of a local sports centre. As The Bannister Sports Centre, this was ultimately opened by the sportsman himself in September 1960.

Swimming is another sport with a considerable local tradition, although boys of Harrow School can be said to have been "in the swim" for at least 100 years longer than Harrow's townsfolk.

As early as 1809, George Butler (best remembered as Byron's Head Master), carried out a major excavation on a tiny pool on land belonging to Lord Northwick off the present Watford Road. Thus began the transformation of the aptly-named "Duck Puddle" into the immensely popular "Ducker", ultimately one of the largest privately-owned pools in Europe.

By the beginning of this century, however, the town was still only at the discussion stage on the provision of a public pool.

One of the most vigorous opponents of the idea was a prospective councillor Henry Samson Clark who, as part of his electoral campaign printed a substantial pamphlet entitled "The Case Against The Baths".

At the time, the town planned both a swimming pool and a slipper bath but Clark felt that the latter, in particular, was a total waste of public money. He argued that since

12 Large towels preserve the modesty of these Harrow School boys at their Ducker pool c.1912 where birthday suits were the normal costume.

13. Another view of Ducker c.1912 in which decency has dictated that the youngster in the middle be given a pair of painted-in bathing trunks of a kind that certainly did not exist some 80 years ago.

14. Only recently demolished, Ducker Cottage, in Watford Road, was originally as dignified a building as you would expect from the architectural practice of the noted Arnold Mitchell.

the town was not a poor district "in the accepted sense", a slipper bath would supply the needs of only those few residents whose homes were without bathrooms.

Whilst it is now impossible to judge the influence exerted by Clark's little publication, the fact remains that Harrow did not get a public swimming pool for another two decades, although the subject was regularly aired in the correspondence of the local press. Many correspondents were unsympathetic if not downright hostile. In June 1911, for example, one resident roundly declared that "if baths are wanted for pleasure, this becomes a luxury and should be paid for by those who have money to throw away". In any event, he reminded his readers, "in August we have the School Ducker open to the public at quite a nominal sum".

Ironically, when Harrow did get a pool, it was largely by accident. Having built a council estate off Lascelles Avenue, it seems that the Local Authority found themselves with a bit of left-over land in what became Charles Crescent, and decided to dig it out as a pool.

There was not even enough money to cart away the tons of excavated earth. Instead, and very fortuitously, the earth was simply banked around the pool's sides, ultimately providing a landscaped setting that (together with the distant view of St. Mary's, Harrow on the Hill), proved to be one of the pool's most popular and attractive features.

Shortly after its opening, the pool was considered good enough to accommodate a British Empire versus the United States Swimming Gala. On this occasion, the American team was captained by none other than Johnny Weissmuller, then fresh from his triumphs in the 1924 Olympics (the Games that inspired the film, "Chariots of Fire") and still some years from his enduring fame as Hollywood's favourite Tarzan.

That Charles Crescent should have secured such a prestigious event was undoubtedly a feather in the cap of the pool's promoters,

15. *Harrow's first outdoor pool in Charles Crescent had the advantage of landscaped gardens and a superb view towards the Hill.*

16. *Wealdstone's later (1934) pool was undoubtedly better designed for swimming but never achieved the same popularity.*

17. A huge inflatable ball was once a feature of Wembley's well patronised swimming pool.

especially as the pool had initially attracted some degree of criticism. At 3ft 6ins, the shallow end was rightly felt to be too deep for the little ones (there was no paddling pool) while, at a mere 7ft, the deep end was not as deep as the town's divers would have wished.

All such drawbacks were taken into account when Harrow acquired its second pool in Christchurch Avenue, Wealdstone, opened by the M.P. Sir Isadore Salmon in May 1934.

Both these pools, of course, have long since been swallowed up by housing developments; even Harrow School's Ducker has been sold off to pay for a more modern indoor pool closer to the School's principal buildings.

Many often amusing memories remain, some prompted by the fact that, given Ducker's tree-shrouded seclusion, generations of boys were able to swim without the encumbrance of costumes. Daphne Rae, a former master's wife, was less than enthusiastic about this tradition.

In her outspoken book *A World Apart*, (which raised quite a few Harrovian eyebrows a decade or so ago), she describes how her husband - a swimming blue - was put in charge of the boys' swimming and how she insisted on accompanying him to the pool. This, of course, meant that swimming costumes suddenly became compulsory, prompting a considerable outcry, not least from Old Harrovians who liked to use the pool. One Old Harrovian Master even decided to ignore the new ruling although, as she wryly comments, he was rarely to be seen other than lying prone upon his stomach!

Inevitably, Ducker has its own Churchill story - of the day when the young and cheeky Winston pushed in a boy of equally small stature, unaware that he was that most revered of beings, a school monitor. Interestingly enough, his victim happened to be Leo Amery who, half a century later, became a member of Churchill's war-time Cabinet.

Raising the Alarm

1. A contemporary lithograph of "The Great Fire Of Harrow" which broke out on a fortunately windless night in October 1838.

There is nothing like a truly catastrophic fire to focus minds on fire protection, and serious concern about the safety of the town's buildings undoubtedly dates from the 1830s, the decade of The Great Fires of Harrow.

While not as famous as the Great Fire of London ("1666 – London burned to sticks"), the Harrow blazes left a very considerable trail of damage; indeed, according to *The Times* report of the second fire in 1838, "Had the wind blown at all fiercely from any quarter, it is probable the whole village would have come down".

Fortunately, the first of the two outbreaks – in January 1831 – was more localised, being confined to the Harrow School boarding house called The Grove which adjoined the parish church.

Six years later, in October 1838, an even bigger blaze consumed the Head Master's House and the adjoining High Street properties. This is an event that is well worth recording at some length, not least for the revealing commentary it offers on human selfishness and folly. It seems that the Harrow School Head Master of the day, Christopher Wordsworth, was continually expressing his resentment at being obliged to share his premises with a number of (presumably noisy) boarders. To relieve him of this nuisance and also, no doubt, to make a little money from boarding fees, one of his masters, Mr Colenso, offered to take the boys into his care.

For this purpose, Colenso built extensive new premises adjoining the Head Master's House in the High Street, bestowing on them all the latest 'mod cons', including an early form of central heating. Shortly after the opening of the house, however, the heating system overheated and ignited the whole property.

2. On the devastated site, the present Head Master's House arose to designs by the famous architect, Decimus Burton - from an 1838 lithograph.

3. Harrow Fire Brigade poses in front of the school house, The Park, in 1883. The little boy was the caller, who in an emergency knocked on the firemen's doors.

4. Harrow's first custom-built fire station, photographed in the 1890s. It was sensibly sited next to the King's Head, whose stables provided horses to draw the engine.

On the alarm being given, two local fire engines rushed to the scene but they were immediately hampered by the fact that the town pump at the top of West Street was under repair. Later, they were joined by machines from London and from Lord Abercorn's Bentley Priory Estate and this augmented force set about pumping water from the then-existing pond in the gardens of The Grove. Simultaneously, Harrow School boys and other volunteers brought water up the hill by means of a bucket chain from The Park lake.

At this stage, however, it was discovered that the hose from The Grove had been damaged, perhaps maliciously. Matters were hardly helped by the actions of Henry Drury, the influential master at the boarding house immediately opposite, who persuaded the firemen to direct their already inadequate water supply onto his own property. Shortly afterwards, and quite without irony, he was able to write to his son: "Thank God, I saved my premises by my own exertions".

Dr Wordsworth and Mr Colenso were not so lucky and their two adjoining houses were quickly and completely gutted. The fire also spread to the neighbouring properties belonging to the town's surgeon, saddler and baker though, fortunately, not to the grocer who was known to have gun-powder in stock!

Not all the losses of the night could be attributed to the fire. Attracted by the flames, which could be seen for miles, looters arrived on the Hill. It was only the hasty swearing-in of a number of special constables, plus the arrival of reinforcements from Bow Street, that enabled some degree of control to be maintained.

With their accommodation destroyed, dozens of boys had to be transferred to other School houses while the Head Master moved into a nearby cottage. There was also a little problem of insurance!

According to another of Drury's surviving letters, the Governors had insured for only £2,800 "and the damage is £5,000 at the least,

5. *William Warren Clowes photographed c.1909 outside the Fire Station with the hose truck he invented some thirty years before.*

6. *Harrow's first motorised fire engine pictured outside the London and Counties Bank (later the Nat West) which adjoined the Fire Station.*

without reference to anything but the building". Some twelve years later, the Hand Book for Harrow On The Hill categorically stated that the premises were insured "partly in The County and partly in The Phoenix Fire Office to about £4,000".

In one aspect, at least, the School seems to have been lucky since the Hand Book further states the "singular fact" that the greater part of the insurance "was only effected a few days before the accident happened".

7. *(far left) The original Fire Station bell and lamp were still in evidence when the latest in motorised engines was photographed in the mid-1930s.*

8. *(left) The Hill Station continued in use with remarkably few changes until 1963.*

9. *(below) Harrow boys watch their boarding house (now West Acre) go up in flames in April 1908 - from a contemporary engraving.*

10. Police, firemen and a few spectators gather outside the still smouldering ruins of the London Road boarding house after the fire of 1908.

The ashes were barely cold when the members of the Harrow Vestry (who numbered fire-fighting among their many public responsibilities) agreed to the cleaning of the local pond and to the purchase of a further fire engine at the not inconsiderable cost of £150.

According to the ever-useful Hand Book, this was originally housed some way from the centre of the town in an engine house in Hogarth Lane (now Crown Street). Three sets of keys were kept with the keeper, at the recently created police station in West Street and at the Crown Inn, virtually opposite the engine house.

It was not until the Local Board of Health assumed responsibility in the 1860s that the engines were moved to a more convenient location in "Mr Cunningham's Yard, Stable and Coach-House in the High Street". This, however, was only a rented property and the Board decided that the best interests of the town could only be met by a custom-built fire station.

Though the author has been unable to identify the exact site and scale of this very first station, it obviously proved inadequate for, around 1866, the Board decided to buy a

11. A lamp post with the word Fire Station marks the entrance to the very first (c.1896) Wealdstone fire establishment - a carriage works in the High Street.

corner plot at the Hill end of Byron Hill Road which was not only suitably central but also convenient to the King's Head Stables (for these, remember, were still the days of horse-drawn fire engines).

On this site, Charles Forster Hayward built the handsome red-brick station (and Board offices) that, in fact, remained in use until the summer of 1963 and, christened The Old Fire Station, still survive as an estate agent's office. Hayward, who also built the town's public hall (where Cafe Cafe now stands) and the school boarding house, Druries, was rarely short of a commission, perhaps because his brother was both a Senior Master at the School and Chairman of the Harrow Board of Health!

When Hayward's station first arose, it had as its neighbours two delightful small properties, Ida Villa and Ivy Cottage. The latter was subsequently bought by the London and Counties Bank who in 1889 put up the premises later occupied by the Nat West and, until their closure in August 1995, the oldest bank premises in the Borough.

In 1895 *The Fireman*, the official organ of the fire service, was able to inform its readers that the Harrow appliances now consisted of "two manual engines, one fire escape, one base-cart especially constructed for the hilly district, one curricle and a good supply of hose, stand-pipes, branch-pipes etc". It also stated that the Brigade consisted of a Chief Officer, 2 foremen, 17 firemen and a resident fireman actually living at the Station.

The same article also commented that a yearly retainer was paid to "the hotel keeper near the fire station" (the King's Head) to keep two horses always available. This, the writer claimed, enabled the Brigade to turn out in a minute and a half.

Given the peculiarities of its site, especially the sharp fall-away of the land, the Hill Station must have been one of the very few of its kind to have the firemen's quarters beneath the engine house; indeed, a serving fire-man once

12. The Wealdstone Brigade, photographed in 1924 outside the Palmerston Road Station with their popular horses, Bob and Nancy, named after the couple who had broken them in for work with the Brigade.

13. Now motorised, the Wealdstone Brigade poses for a picture in the late 1920s.

memorably remarked that the Harrow firemen were the only team to go "up the pole" whenever the fire-bell rang!

Other fire stations followed in the district, of which the Wealdstone station sprang from a local disaster. In 1895 an old lady stumbled as she carried a burning oil lamp upstairs in her little shop on Wealdstone railway bridge and soon set the premises ablaze.

A messenger was quickly sent on horseback to alert the Harrow Brigade while passers by tackled the flames with equipment borrowed from the railway station but, thinking he had seen a runaway horse, a cart-driver attempted to block the road, causing the Wealdstone messenger to be thrown. Rather than risk similar accidents in the future, Wealdstone residents volunteered to create their own brigade and this was officially formed in August 1896.

Originally housed in a small corrugated iron building in the High Street, the Wealdstone engine was subsequently moved to Palmerston Road, where it was pulled by two notably hard-working horses, called Bob and Nancy. The rest of their time was apparently spent pulling the local refuse cart!

Pinner, too, was also obliged to open a Fire Brigade Fund around 1880 in order to maintain its own firefighters following a disastrous fire at a confectioners.

Without in any way attempting a roll-call of notable Harrow fires, it may be worth recalling that two Wealdstone factories – Cogswell and Harrison and David Allen – were badly damaged in fires in respectively 1894 and 1912.

Harrow School has also seen rather more than its fair share of blazes, including the total destruction of the boarding house now called West Acre in London Road in April 1908. Most of the time it housed some 48 boys but, happily, at the hour of the outbreak, they were virtually all attending a lecture in Speech Room.

14. The Pinner Brigade, founded in 1880, was some 10 years old when G. Beaumont Senior posed with the Pinner Fire Engine in a yard in Waxwell Lane.

In Sickness and in Health

1. The Hill's first custom-built cottage hospital was this neat Victorian villa in Lower Road.

Harrow has traditionally been regarded as a healthier place than many of its lower-lying neighbours. Over the centuries it is known to have been a refuge from the plagues and ills that beset London; for example, in 1537, Richard Layton, then Rector of Harrow, was able to promise his mentor, Thomas Cromwell, twenty beds in the town "where there has been no sickness in a year".

Judging from many subsequent memoirs, parents of Harrow School boys were also much attracted to the notion of "high and healthy Harrow".

The tradition persists even to this day. The old-style coat-of-arms to which the Borough has

2. After nearly 90 years, the frontage of Arnold Mitchell's Cottage Hospital on Roxeth Hill remains almost completely unchanged.

recently reverted features a berobed female figure representing Hygeia, the Goddess of Health.

Even the healthiest of towns, however, must have its occasional disease and accident victims and, in default of any earlier records, we know that in 1773, two public-spirited parishioners of St. Mary's, Harrow on the Hill, caused a small infirmary – or pest house – to be built on Sudbury Common. This was specifically intended for "such poor persons as should be afflicted with infectious diseases or labour under dangerous accidents".

Three quarters of a century later, the Sudbury pest-house had become so dilapidated that demolition seemed the only solution, adding further weight to the then-current arguments for a new and 'modern' hospital.

This duly opened in February 1866, although, in truth, the building was not a custom-built hospital but a conversion from two cottages (Vine Cottages) on Roxeth Hill. It offered nine beds only.

There was only one paid nurse, the rest of the work being carried out by a voluntary team led

3. A 1920s portrait of the staff of Harrow Hospital outside the handsome front entrance of the building erected in 1906.

4. Diana Churchill, daughter of Sir Winston Churchill, arrives to open the Florence Nightingale Nurses Home in October, 1930.

by Constance Hewlett, daughter of Thomas Hewlett, the town doctor who himself had done so much to improve the town's drainage and sanitation some 17 years before. The building, however, had been secured only on a short-term lease and, two years later, the landlady gave them notice to quit.

Happily, a local benefactor called Charles Leaf came to the rescue with the offer of a piece of land in Lower Road – providing the necessary money could be found for a new hospital building. Fund raising then continued until 1872 when Harrow's first custom-built hospital opened its doors. It was known as the 'cottage' hospital although, in truth, as our drawing reveals, it looked more like a fair-sized private house (a villa perhaps) than a cottage.

Staffing was obviously still a problem for "as far as circumstances will allow" patients were required to be responsible for their own laundry. They were also expected to assist in housework, needlework, gardening and similar chores.

If this gave rise to complaint, it obviously had to be expressed with notable restraint for a list of rules printed in the 1896 Cottage Hospital Report declares that "profane, abusive and immoral language or behaviour will be punished by dismissal from the house".

Even the patients' reading was vetted, as yet another rule lays down that "the nurse will allow no book or publication in the wards, except such as are sanctioned by the Vicar of Harrow".

From the same source we learn that, in 1895, the hospital cared for a total of 78 patients (19 more than the previous year) at an average weekly cost of £1.6s.10d (about £1.35).

In those days, of course, all patients were required to pay for hospital treatment although the scale of charges tried to take into account an individual's financial circumstances. The "labouring classes", as they were dubbed, paid only ninepence a day whereas small shop-keepers or mechanics were asked for one shilling (5p). Interestingly enough, domestic servants, of which there would have been many

5. Some time after the opening of the new wing in 1932, nurses enjoy a snow-ball battle.

6. Based at Stanmore since 1909, the Royal National Orthopaedic Hospital constructed open-ended wards at Brockley Hill in 1922 for the care of tubercular children.

in the affluent Hill community, were expected to pay more, the cost presumably being borne by their employers.

Though even the highest of these charges seems low to us today, 120 years ago they were considered substantial enough to require every patient to sign a paper guaranteeing payment of "the sum required for maintenance".

The day scheduled for the opening of the new cottage hospital turned out to be "one of the wettest days of the wettest season in the memory of men", so comparatively few of the general public took up the invitation to inspect the 11 beds, two resident staff rooms, the operating room and dispensary. The local press, however, turned up and subsequently admired "the extremely pretty views" up the Hill from the wards.

Only days before this opening, it appears that Constance Hewlett, now the (voluntary) Lady Manager, discovered that the builders had somehow failed to provide a wash-house so she hastily converted the intended mortuary; the coal-house then became the mortuary!

Right from the start, in fact, the building had serious disadvantages. Some years later, one of its original physicians, Dr. A.H. Williams, wrote that it was difficult to believe that it had ever been designed as a hospital since the wards were small and inconvenient and on several floors. The staircase, he also complained, was steep and narrow "so that it was impossible to carry patients to the upper floors with safety and comfort".

In any event, its facilities were quickly overstretched by the demands of the fast-growing Harrow community, not least for the treatment of infectious diseases.

As early as 1885 the always precarious finances of the Lower Road hospital had been badly shaken by the inadvertent admission of a small-pox victim. This meant that an entire ward had to be repainted and white-washed and its bedding and furniture renewed.

The obvious solution was to build a separate isolation hospital and in 1894, a small specialist unit arose in Roxbourne primarily "for the

7. *Happily there were more nurses than children when Harrow Hospital's children's ward was photographed one Christmas between the two World Wars.*

reception of cases of scarlet fever, diphtheria, enteric fever and Asiatic cholera".

Inevitably, its rules had to be even more stringent than those of the Cottage Hospital. Visits, in particular, were strictly controlled both in time (two afternoons a week) and duration (no more than 15 minutes) and then "only in special circumstances with the sanction of the Medical Officer or the Sanitary Inspector will they be allowed to enter the ward".

Patients, however, might have been able to take some comfort from the dietary list which, as published in 1895, allowed those on the so-called 'full diet' some four ounces of suet pudding, three times a week!

Around this time, too, plans were laid for a much bigger general hospital. The chosen architect was the much-admired Arnold Mitchell (who also designed Orley Farm School) and his graceful building still stands at the top of Roxeth Hill. Once described as the prettiest cottage hospital in the country, it was much extended over the years, the Queen Mother (then Duchess of York), helping her husband to open a major extension in 1932.

In 1933 it achieved recognition as a training school for nurses but the influx of student nurses created accommodation problems that were partly solved by the acquisition of the old Roxeth Vicarage on the adjoining site. Subsequently, other buildings were added, including the Edith Martin Memorial Hall in memory of a highly regarded matron who died suddenly in 1963.

Arnold Mitchell's building still serves the district's elderly sick but its primary role has long since been assumed by the vast Northwick Park Hospital in Watford Road which our present Queen opened in 1970.

Interested readers should be warned that there is little point in seeking out the Lower Road Hospital. It became a private house called "The Retreat" and was destroyed by a bomb during World War II.

Going Downhill

1 In the early decades of this century, No. 41 High Street, Harrow on the Hill, the premises between the two shops, was the town's principal Post Office.

Harrow must be one of the very few towns where the phrase "going downhill" has usually meant improvement rather than the reverse. This was especially apparent in the early years of this century when, one by one, most of the town's public services moved down to Greenhill from the (literally) narrow confines of The Hill, previously the true centre of the town.

Thus it was that, in 1914, down-the-hill Greenhill got a handsome custom-built main Post Office in College Road more or less on

2. Staff line up outside Stanmore Hill Post Office early this century while two men (possibly Berwick and son) stand in the doorway of the adjoining shop.

the site of the present Post Office in place of the old Harrow High Street premises. The Harrow Observer commented at the time: "There has been a tendency for businesses to migrate from the scholastic heights to the commercial lands of the lower ground and the GPO are only moving with the times."

The High Street building, which had opened in 1879, was by no means the first Post Office on the Hill. In 1852 a house on Church Hill owned by James Woodbridge served this purpose; indeed, by 1867, there was an official Post Master for the area who employed four letter-carriers, two railway messengers and a so-called rural messenger. Over and above their wages, the letter-carriers each received an allowance of three (old) pence to buy oil for their "breast-lamps", although only between the 'dark' months of October and April.

Earlier still, the inn-keeper John Bliss maintained a post office at the Crown and Anchor Inn, situated right next door to Harrow School's gates. Here mail coach called twice a day, enabling Bliss to make two daily deliveries.

By 1850 the Hand Book to Harrow On The Hill could actually promise those contemplating residence on the Hill that letters posted in London before 9 o'clock in the morning would be delivered by 12 noon; similarly, letters catching

3. *Wembley Post Office and Telegraph Office in the High Road some time before 1906 when a new Post Office was opened across the road.*

4. *Still affectionately remembered by many residents, the former College Road Post Office stood on the same site as today's much larger building.*

5. An original pen and ink drawing of the first Cunningham Building Society's office in London Road, Harrow on the Hill. The building still exists but with an altered frontage.

the 3 o'clock afternoon post in London would be delivered before six that night. There was also an overnight service which guaranteed delivery by breakfast time of all letters posted by 8.00p.m. the previous evening. These letter-carriers do not appear to have adopted the name "post-men" until some time in the 1880s, about the time that the Harrow Gazette published a heartfelt plea on their behalf. "If each house-holder were to provide a letter-box", the paper declared, "it would save much time and avoid needless delay".

Though Greenhill had to wait until 1914 for its own principal Post Office - on land that was once occupied by the houses Hawarden Lodge and The Chestnuts - there had been sub-post offices in local retailers for 40 years or more, including one in Peterborough Road and another next to The Havelock Arms public house in Station Road.

These little shops were invariably well patronised, the press commenting early in 1914 that one of their number had sold no less than £160 worth of stamps - then a very considerable sum - the previous Christmas.

In the event, the phenomenal growth of the town soon put even the new College Road Post Office under severe pressure and, by 1938, major improvements had been planned. These, however, were inevitably halted by the outbreak of World War II and it was not until 1958 that building work began.

Since the postal service could not be interrupted, temporary offices were set up on the site of what is now Northwick Park Hospital and a temporary counter service offered in Station Road. The job was finally completed at the end of 1961 and the nucleus of what we now regard as Harrow Post Office opened in the summer of 1962.

Another long-established Hill service that ultimately moved downhill was Harrow's very first - indeed, very own - building society. Originally known as the Cunningham Permanent Building Society, it was founded in 1882 by John William Cunningham, son of Harrow's famous Victorian vicar whose names he shared. He ran an adult Bible class and his aim seems to have been to

6. *The well-remembered Cunningham House on the corner of Bessborough Road and Roxborough Avenue was demolished in 1973 to make way for a modern office block.*

7. *The staff of Pinner Post Office photographed around the turn of the century.*

8. Until pipes were put down by the Harrow Waterworks Company, whose depot was down the hill in Bessborough Road, most of the Hill's water came from this pump house at the top of West Street.

encourage the young working men he taught to save towards the acquisition of their own homes.

At first, the company was too small to require full-time premises. Instead, it operated from the Hill's Literary Institute, then in a surviving building next door to Hill and Saunders, the School's photographers. Here monies were received every Monday evening from 8.00 to 9.00p.m. while the Secretary was available to give advice between 8.00 and 10.00p.m. on Tuesday evenings.

In the first annual statement, it was reported that £1,400 had been received from investors and that £950 had been advanced on "four satisfactory mortgages". Of this total, £450 was advanced to a Mr P.G. Walter (no relation of the author!) for the purchase of a property in Middle Road.

From this relatively slow start, the company steadily prospered and, earlier this century, larger permanent premises were sought. Inevitably, they were found down the Hill in a Victorian villa in Bessborough Road. It was called Harcourt House but this was promptly changed to Cunningham House.

In 1939, the company itself was renamed the Harrow Building Society - the name that the modest Cunningham had originally wanted but had been unable to register since there was an existing society in the 1880s that bore a somewhat similar designation.

Although hit by a land mine during World War II, Cunningham House actually survived into the 1970s when it was demolished to make way for a modern office block. As for the Society itself, it too changed its name. As the Birmingham and Mid-Shires Society, it still has offices in Station Road, Harrow, as well as in Pinner, Stanmore and Eastcote.

It would be geographically correct to say that the local police also moved downhill, although, in truth, the Hill Police Station was never more than a couple of hundred yards up West Street.

Right from the start (in January 1840 when the Metropolitan Police was obliged to take Harrow

9. Although there had been a station of sorts on the slopes of Harrow Hill since the 1840s, these Wealdstone and Stanmore bobbies did not get a proper station of their own until two years after this 1907 photograph.

10. Local government offices remained on the Hill longer than most; indeed, this beautiful Council Chamber was built for the old Harrow Urban District Council as late as 1914. It still survives within the business premises at 90, High Street.

11. Our local paper also started on the Hill. William Winkley was the first owner but it was William Overhead (whose premises can be seen on the left) who transformed it from a small monthly to a large-format weekly.

into its care), a rented cottage seems to have served as a police house at the lower end of West Street. This was, of course, some distance from the existing hill-top town and, in June 1866, the Harrow Gazette welcomed a proposal to provide new police accommodation further up the Hill in Crown Street. "The present situation", they wrote, "is too far in case of emergency". Instead, that same year, the Police Commissioners purchased the freehold of their original site.

Eight years later, the Gazette was bemoaning not only the location but the delapidation of the station. "Considering the large amount paid for Police Rate (nearly £1,900 a year)", an editorial declared, "we think we should have as respectable looking a building as we see in other parishes of less importance".

This "respectable looking building" – the building that is still used today by traffic wardens – finally arrived in 1873, giving the town a full 90 years of police service before a new station was opened in Northolt Road, South Harrow.

Among the very last to quit the Hill were our Local Government officers. 1914 (the same year that saw the move of The Post Office) also witnessed the building of a handsome new office for the then Harrow Urban District Council. This was right next door to the earlier Board offices in the Fire Station building and, amazingly enough, it was still being used by Harrow's Education Department as late as 1963.

An even older survivor has been the Hill's one-and-only bank, the London and County Bank, more recently a branch of the National Westminster. First opened in 1862, the bank moved to improved premises at 47 High Street in 1873, then moved across the road to its present custom-built building in 1891.

Largely through the patronage of generations of Harrow School boys, it managed to remain in business for a further century. But, in August 1995, the bank's customers were informed that the doors would soon be shutting forever and that all business would be transferred – down the hill to the branch in Station Road.

Royal Occasions

1. Queen Victoria's "surprise" visit to Harrow in 1848, as recorded for the pages of the Illustrated London News.

Even in these egalitarian times, a visit by Royalty is guaranteed to draw a large and eager crowd so it is not difficult to imagine the excitement engendered in the little town of Harrow by the many Royal visits of the past.

The very first such visit, in 1804, appears to have been entirely spontaneous, the often-unpredictable George III having decided to drive over from his castle at Windsor. Entirely without warning, he appears to have alighted from his carriage outside the old Crown and

Anchor inn, which then stood right next to the entrance gates to Old Schools.

According to Percy M. Thornton's 1885 history, John Bliss, the landlord "thought to exalt Harrow in the good King's eyes by producing a local sprig of nobility". But, on the prompt arrival of the Duke of Dorset, the monarch was doubtlessly surprised to find himself in the company of a very small and possibly very nervous Duke, who just happened to be a pupil at the School.

Ultimately, it was left to Lord Northwick, then living in the house we now call The Park in the High Street, to entertain the King who was properly complimentary about the fine views of London from its grounds.

As it proved, it was a further 44 years before a reigning monarch was to return to Harrow. Again, the visit was largely informal, Queen Victoria having expressed a wish to visit Harrow in the course of a short stay at nearby Bentley Priory, then the residence of the Queen Dowager.

Presumably some notice was got to Harrow for, although the Illustrated London News claimed that Her Majesty's intention had not been known to the inhabitants, "till the same morning, triumphal arches had been erected as if by magic".

On investigation, the magic appears to have had a solidly practical base, as a handwritten subscription list in the Harrow Local History Collection reveals. This intriguing discovery begins: "A considerable expense having been incurred in erecting the Triumphal Arches, the hire of banners etc... an appeal is made to all loyal inhabitants for the purpose of discharging the same".

It seems that a number of the town's leading residents and traders duly obliged. Among them, with a contribution of ten shillings (50p), was a certain Mr Bliss, just possibly an offspring of the very same man who had greeted King George some four decades earlier.

2. On Speech Day, 1894, Harrow boys and their guests wait by a splendidly decorated Speech Room for the arrival of the Prince and Princess of Wales (later Edward and Alexandra).

3. Eleven years later in 1905, King Edward VII, as the Prince had become, returned with his Queen to celebrate Harrow School's acquisition of its present Football Fields.

4. In an open carriage, King Edward VII passes by cheering crowds in June 1905.

As was to be expected, the Queen and Prince Albert were shown over Harrow School. Much more interestingly – and, indeed, this may well have been a particular reason for the visit – the Royal party also toured St. Mary's, which had only just undergone an almost total transformation at the hands of the increasingly famous architect, George Gilbert Scott.

Prince Albert, accompanied by the Prince of Wales, returned to Harrow School for Speech Day in 1894. A year later, the Prince Consort travelled by train – a comparatively new experience – to the opening of the Royal Commercial Travellers School at Hatch End (of which only the Elliott Hall now survives). Unhappily – and one can readily imagine the embarrassment of the railway officials – the train was at least twenty minutes late and a large and fashionable assembly was kept waiting in some suspense. An unforgiving Harrow Gazette firmly attributed the delay to "the mismanagement of the railway".

5. Edward VII also paid several visits privately to the neighbourhood, most notably to Warren House, Stanmore, in June 1907 to visit his friends the Bischoffsheims.

6. Families gather in a suitably decorated Pinner High Street for the start of a street parade to mark the Coronation of King George V in 1911.

7. *Coronation Day (June 22, 1911) also saw a colourful parade of decorated carts in Wealdstone High Street.*

A comparable misfortune seems to have fallen Victoria's heir, Edward VII, on a private visit to Stanmore in 1907. His hosts on this occasion were the Bischoffsheims who lived in great style at the still surviving Warren House in Wood Lane.

En route to Stanmore, with only a single equerry in attendance, the Royal car broke down not once but twice and the King arrived in time for tea rather than the intended luncheon party. Probably because his special friend, Mrs George Keppel, was also on the guest list, the King consented to stay for dinner; indeed, according to the local paper, "the car swung through Stanmore on its return journey as the parish clock pointed the hour of midnight".

By an interesting coincidence, the King also formed a strong attachment to Agnes Keyser, daughter of the family from whom the Bischoffsheims acquired Warren House. He was, in fact, dining with Agnes Keyser on the very night in 1901 on which he was obliged to rush to Osborne House to the bedside of the

8. *"As we welcomed the father, so we welcome the son", read this banner put up in Harrow's High Street to mark the visit of King George V to Harrow School in 1912.*

9. *On the same 1912 occasion, guests arrive at Speech Room, as imposingly decorated as it was in 1894 (possibly with the same decorations!).*

10. *The bearded King, followed by a magnificently behatted Queen Mary, crosses from the Vaughan Library accompanied by Head Master of Harrow, the Rev. Lionel Ford.*

11. *The Duke of York (soon to be King George VI) uses a golden key to open the Stuart wing of Harrow Hospital in memory of former hospital president, J.N. Stuart.*

dying Queen Victoria. Agnes Keyser also seems to have been the very last person to entertain her sovereign since they dined together at her London home on 2 May 1910, just four days before his death.

For all the King's fondness for attractive and intelligent women (and Agnes Keyser was both), it seems likely that they were drawn together by a mutual interest in the care of the sick and wounded. Agnes Keyser preferred to be known as Sister Agnes and, during the Boer War, turned her home into a military nursing home (from which ultimately grew the renowned King Edward VII Hospital for Officers).

Edward VII, while still Prince of Wales, had earlier paid an official visit to Harrow School for Speech Day, 1894, an event well recorded by the photographers of the day. When, in turn, his son George V paid a similar visit in 1912, the town paid him a singularly graceful compliment by draping a banner across the main thoroughfare reading: "As we welcomed the father so we welcome the son". Appropriately enough, given its position virtually outside the fire station, the banner

12. Bridge Street, Pinner is bedecked with flags to commemorate the 1937 Coronation of King George VI, father of our present Queen.

13. The popular Prince of Wales, later King Edward VIII, is shown the historic Peachey Stone by Vicar Edgar Stogden during a visit to Harrow Hill in 1923.

14. (top) Queen Mary, photographed with Vicar Geoffrey Woolley, when she paid a totally spontaneous visit to St. Mary's Church in 1950.

15. (above) In 1954 Harrow, formerly an Urban District, received its Charter of Incorporation as a Borough from the present Queen's uncle, the Duke of Gloucester. Seated nearby is Prime Minister Clement Attlee, then a Stanmore resident.

was suspended from two of the Brigade's extension ladders.

Thirty-eight years later, Queen Mary emulated George III's example by turning up on the Hill – at St. Mary's Church – totally unannounced. The Vicar of the day, Geoffrey Woolley, was speaking on the phone when his wife handed him a note reading "Queen Mary wants to see you". Initially he thought he was the victim of a joke but, there on the doorstep, was indeed the familiar figure, accompanied only by a lady-in-waiting.

Apparently, Queen Mary had been in the district and felt it would be nice to see again the building an earlier monarch, King Charles II, had dubbed "the most visible church".

To bring our story of Royal occasions up-to-date (without claim to be a complete record of all such Royal events), our present Queen has found time for frequent visits to the Hill (in 1957, 1971, and 1986) and, most memorably, down the hill, in 1970 when she performed the opening of Northwick Park Hospital.

16. *Privileged onlookers crowd St. Mary's Vicarage garden as the young Queen Elizabeth II walks up Church Hill with Head Master of Harrow, Robert James, in 1957.*

17. *The Queen also found time for a brief visit to St. Mary's and a meeting with Vicar Guy Whitcombe.*

18. The Queen performs the official opening ceremony of Northwick Park Hospital and Research Centre in October 1970.

19. The Queen greets Head Master Ian Beer and his wife in 1986 when she laid the foundation stone of the Churchill Schools on Grove Hill.

Index

Alexandra Avenue 26
Amateur Athletics Association 158
Amery, Leo 162
Archbishop Anselm 134
Architects –
    F.E. Bromige 110
    Decimus Burton 164
    Charles Forster Hayward 172
    Arnold Mitchell 76, 176, 182
    E.S. Prior 60
Army & Navy Stores 46
Attlee, Clement 200
"A World Apart" 162

Baldwin, Stanley 54
Balfour, Betty 107
Ball, Alan 64
Band of Mercy 76
Bannister, Sir Roger 156, 158
Bannister Sports Centre 158
Baptist Mission 29
Beaumont, George 174
Becket, Archbishop Thomas 136
Beerhouse Act 116
Bentley Priory 12, 77, 132, 165, 192
Bentley Priory Circular Walk 64
Bessborough Road, Harrow 24, 117, 144, 187, 188
Betz, Pauline 157
Bischoffsheim family 195, 198
Birmingham & Midshires Building Society 188
Blackwell, Charles 62, 64
Blackwell, Thomas 64
Bliss, John 118, 184, 192
Bonnersfield Lane, Harrow 85
Brabazon of Tara, Lord 48
Bridge Street, Pinner 95, 108, 111, 112, 198
Brooks, Albert 106
Brookshill 64
Builders –
    Comben & Wakeling 28, 42
    Fk. & Charles Costain 28
    Alfred Cutler & Sons 28
    Laing Estates 28
    T.F. Nash 24, 26, 28, 40, 41
    Harry Neal 28
    E.S. Reed 28
Burns Road, Sudbury 99
Byrkhede, John 136
Byron Hill Road, Harrow 142, 172
Byron Road, Wealdstone 36

Cafe Cafe 172
Carl Rosa Opera Company 114
Carson, Sir Edward 54
Chapel Lane, Pinner 95
"Chariots of Fire" 160
Charles Crescent, Harrow 28, 160, 161
Charter of Incorporation 200
Christchurch Avenue, Wealdstone 162
Churches –
    All Saints, Harrow Weald 138, 143, 151
    Bessborough Road Methodist Church 146
    Christ Church, Roxeth 138, 146
    Church of Our Lady & St Thomas of Canterbury ..
    .... 144, 148

    College Road Baptist Church 89, 146
    Harrow Welsh Church 144
    Holy Trinity, Wealdstone 148
    St Lawrence, Whitchurch 132
    St John's, Greenhill 140, 145
    St John's, Pinner 96, 113, 136, 143
    St John's, Wembley 138
    St Mary's, Harrow on the Hill 12, 66, 116, 131,
    ..132, 133, 134,136, 137, 139, 139, 141, 142, 160,
    176, 200
    St Peter's, West Harrow 148
    Stanmore Old Church 136, 143
Church Fields 149
Church Hill, Harrow 66, 80, 201
Churchill, Diana 177
Churchill Schools 202
Churchill, Sir Winston 162, 177
Church Lane, Pinner 50
Church Road, Stanmore 47
Cinemas –
    Broadway, Harrow 92, 104
    Coronet, Wealdstone 103-106
    Dominion/Cannon/Safari, Harrow 90, 110
    Elite/Cosy/Carlton, Harrow Hill 108
    Embassy, North Harrow 17, 107, 112
    Granada/Cannon, Harrow 85, 110
    Gaumont State, Kilburn 88
    Grosvenor, Rayners Lane 26, 109, 110
    Harrow Coliseum 84, 90, 105-107, 112
    Herga, Wealdstone 108
    Langham, Pinner 108, 112
    Odeon, Kenton 110
    Odeon, Kingsbury 110
    Odeon, South Harrow 110
    Odeon, Wealdstone 110
    Odeon, Wembley 109, 110
    Picturedrome, Harrow 102-104
    Rowley's Coliseum & Picture House, Wealdstone ..
    102
    Star Theatre, Wealdstone 102
"The City" 62, 64
Clark Henry Sampson 158
Clarke & Co 14, 88
Clowes William Warrent 167
Clutterbuck Brewery 126, 127
Cocoa Tree Temperance Tavern 125
College Hill Road, Harrow Weald 36
College Road, Harrow 15, 84, 86, 88, 89
College Road, Harrow Weald 99, 129
College Road Post Office 183, 185
Common Road, Harrow Weald 44
Copland, Anne & Frances 138
"The Countryside Lies Sleeping" 64
Cromwell, Oliver 124
Cromwell, Thomas 175
Crosse & Blackwell 64
Cunningham Building Society 186
Cunningham House 187, 188
Cunningham, John William 186
Cunningham, the Rev. John 8, 66, 115, 138, 140, 144

Daimler Wagonette 43, 46
Denville, Sir Alfred 112, 114
Domesday Book 7, 131, 132

Dorset, Duke of 192
Douglas Avenue, Wembley 42

Ealing Road, Sudbury 99
Eastcote Lane, South Harrow 24
Elm Park, Stanmore 33
English Place Name Society 62
Esdaile, Alfred 114
Express Supermarkets 114

Factories –
    David Allen (later HMSO)..............52, 57, 58, 174
    Cogswell & Harrison 52, 174
    Hamilton's Brush Works 52
    Kodak Ltd 40, 51-56, 152
    Little Laundry Ltd 58-60
    Roxeth Gas Works 61, 62
    Whitefriars Glass Works 52
    Winsor & Newton 52
Farmborough family 116, 119
Farms – Barnetts Farm 26
    Durrants Farm 25
    Honeyburn Farm 24
    Kenton Grove Farm 100
    Moat Farm (Headstone Manor) 27
    Rayners Farm 25
    Roxeth Farm 25, 26
    Weald Farm 23
"The Fireman" 172
"First Four Minutes" 158

Gaiety Theatre 114
Gayton Rooms 84
Gerrard William 135
Gilbert, W.S. 44
Gloucester, Duke of 200
Goodall, Frederick 64
Gordon, Frederick 12
Gordon Avenue, Stanmore 14
Gore Spencer 152
Graham Road, Wealdstone 103
Grange Road, South Harrow 29, 62
Green & Edwards 88
Greenhill of Harrow, Lord 50
Greenhill Parade, Station Road 82
Greenhill, Samuel 46
Grim's Dyke, Harrow Weald 44
Grove Hill, Harrow 43, 44, 46, 202
Gunn, Marie 42

Hadow, P.F. (Frank) 152
Hall, Florence 106
Handbook to Harrow Hill 80, 168, 170, 184
"Harrow Before Your Time" 14
Harrow Civic Centre 73
Harrow Fire Brigade 165, 169
Harrow Garden Village 28
Harrow Gazette 43, 144, 186, 190, 194
Harrow Horse Committee 50
Harrow Hospital 1778, 179, 181
Harrow Marathon 153
Harrow Observer 104, 154
Harrow Local History Collection 7, 149, 192
Harrow Public Hall 108
Harrow Recreation Ground 153, 156
Harrow & Roxeth Dispensary 74
Harrow School –
    Bradbys 72, 152
    Chapel 138, 146
    Churchill Schools 202

Custos 118
Druries 80, 172
Ducker 158, 159, 162
Ducker Cottage 160
Football Fields 193
The Grove 163
Head Master's House 164
Old Schools 116, 140, 192
Laundry 56, 60
John Lyon 66, 138, 149
Wm & Joseph Mason 150
The Park 166, 192
Richard Brinsley Sheridan 150
Silver Arrow Tournament 150, 152
Sixth Form Cricket Ground 151
Sir Gilbert Talbot 150
Speech Room 174, 193, 197
The Rev. Torre 8
Vaughan Library 115, 146
War Memorial Building 80
West Acre 169, 170, 174
Harrow School Masters –
    Ian Beer 2 02
    George Butler 158
    Mr Colenso 164, 165
    Henry Drury 165
    Rev. Lionel Ford 197
    Benjamin Heath 152
    Robert James 201
    Rev. A.G. Phelps 10
    Charles Vaughan 68
    Rev. A.G. Watson 56, 164
    Dr. Joseph Wood 44
    Christopher Wordsworth 164, 165
Harrow Urban District Council 189, 190
Harrow Waterworks Co. 188
Harrow Weald Recreation Ground 64
Hartley, Rev. John 152
Havelock Place 71
Headstone Drive 40, 52, 57
Headstone Lane 38
Headstone Manor 27
Herga Lawn Tennis Club 156
Hewlett, Constance 178, 180
Hewlett, Marion 68, 74, 76, 78
Hewlett, Thomas 74, 178
High Road, Harrow Weald 23, 25
High Street, Harrow on the Hill 183, 184, 189
Hills & Saunders 188
Honeypot Lane, Stanmore 35
Horsenden Hill 130
Horsley, Gerald 11

Iceland Supermarket 107, 112
Ida Villa 172
Iffley Road, Oxford 156
Illustrated London News 191, 192
Imperial Drive, North Harrow 18
Imperial Electric Carriage 48
Isleworth Church 131
Ivy Cottage 172

Jayne, Miss E.B. 58, 59
Johnson, Ben 124

Kenmare House 85
Kenton Lane 33, 47. 122
Kenton Park Avenue 24, 100
Kenton Road 24
Kepple, Mrs George 196

Keyser, Agnes	196, 198
Kiln House	64
Kiln Nursery & Garden Centre	64
Knotts Carriage Works	63
King Edward VII Hospital	198
Lascelles Avenue	160
Laud, Archbishop William	136
Layton, Richard	175
Leabourne Manufacturing Company	154
Leaf, Charles	178
Lindfield, Henry	48
Lloyd George, David	58
London & Birmingham Railway	7, 122
London & Counties Bank	167, 172, 190
London Evening News Marathon	153
London General Omnibus Co.	47
London & North Western Railway	45, 46
London Road, Harrow on the Hill	186
London Road, Stanmore	34
Lower Road, Harrow	175, 180
Lowlands Road	16, 69, 71, 86, 155
Lowlands Villa	69, 71, 72
Lyson's "Environs of London"	149
Manning, Cardinal	144
Manor of Little Stanmore	132
Manor Parade, Station Road	85
Marlborough Road, Wealdstone	13
Marsh Road, Pinner	95
Martin, Edith	182
Masonic Lodges	84
Masons Avenue, Wealdstone	93
Matthews, Jessie	110
Metropolitan Police	188
Metropolitan Railway	12, 15, 16, 26
Middle Road, Harrow	68, 78, 116
Middlesex Regiment	126
Mount Park Estate	14
National Westminster Bank	167, 172, 190
Nelson Road	118, 120
Nicholl, Jean (Mrs Bostock)	156, 157
Nobes Forge	63
Northolt Airport	60, 62
Northolt Road, South Harrow	14, 30, 31, 32, 58, 61, 90-92, 119, 190
Northumberland Road	28
Northwick, Pinner & District Hospital	28
Northwick, the Barons	8, 66, 158
Northwick Park Hospital	182, 186, 202
Old Berkeley Hunt	34
Old Redding	62, 64, 122, 126, 129
Olympic Games	152, 154, 160
Osborne House	198
Overhead, William	190
Oxford Road, Harrow	87
Paddington-Greenford Canal	142
"The Paddocks"	31
Palmerston Road, Wealdstone	174
Patch, Wally	104
Peck, Hon. W.	148
Perry, Fred	156
Peets, Rev. W. H.	151
Peterborough Road, Harrow	82, 87, 88, 186
Piccadilly Line	26
Pinner Fair	111, 113
Pinner Fire Brigade	174

Pinner Post Office	96, 187, 195
Pinner Road	28, 38, 87, 154
Plowden, Edmund	124
Pope, W. MacQueen	114
Port, Thomas	10
Public Houses –	
Abercorn Arms	127
Ballot Box	130
Bricklayers Arms	120
The Case is Altered	62, 122, 128, 129
The Castle	120
The Cricketers	118, 120, 122
The Crown	120
Crown Inn	47
Crown & Anchor	115, 116, 184, 192
Duck in the Pond	42, 122
Half Moon	119, 120
Havelock Arms	92, 186
Kingsfield Arms	117
King's Head	12, 58, 84, 108, 116, 118, 120, 165, 172
Lord Nelson	120
Marquis of Granby	85, 86
North Star	120
Queen's Head	124, 125
Red Lion	129, 130
Rest Hotel	123
Rose & Crown	122
Royal Oak	102, 121
Seven Balls	47
Three Horseshoes	16, 60, 119
Timber Carriage	94
The Vine	49
White Hart	120
White Horse	116
Public Schools Act	68
Rae, Daphne	162
Rayners Lane	26, 37-41
"The Retreat", Lower Road	182
Riches, Major	46
Robertson, Max	154
Rotch, Benjamin	69, 71
Rotch, Isabella	68
Roxborough Avenue	187
Roxborough Bridge	88, 153
Roxbourne Hospital	180, 182
Roxeth Barn	27
Roxeth Corner	63, 67, 90, 119, 155
Roxeth Hill	66, 119, 144, 176
Roxeth Marathon	155
Roxeth Vicarage	182
Royal National Orthopaedic Hospital	179
Royalty – Prince Albert	194
King Charles II	136
King Edward VII	193, 194-198
King Edward VIII	199
Queen Elizabeth I	149
Queen Elizabeth II	182, 201, 202
Elizabeth The Queen Mother	182
King George III	191
King George V	195, 198
King George VI	197, 198
King Henry VIII	118
Louise, Princess	76
Queen Mary	200
Queen Victoria	76, 191, 192, 194
King William I	7, 131
Salmon, Sir Isadore	162

St Anne's Road, Harrow 71, 78, 81, 82, 86
St Leonard's Avenue, Kenton..................................24
Scott, George Gilbert 133, 146, 194
Scott, Peter G 12
Sewell, Edwin 46, 48
Schools (other than Harrow School)
    Bridge Schools, Wealdstone......................73-75
    Grant Road School, Wealdstone 73
    Greenhill College, ...69
    Greenhill School, Harrow..........................71, 72
    Harrow Girls' County School.....................68, 69
    Harrow Technical College 69, 106
    John Lyon School 68, 78
    Otley Farm School, Harrow 76, 182
    Roxeth Hill School 65, 68, 78
    Royal Commercial Travellers Schools 194
    St Andrew's College, Harrow Weald.................129
    St Dominic's, Harrow on the Hill....................144
    St Margaret's, Harrow 156
    Welldon Park School, South Harrow 67
    Whitefriars School, Wealdstone 75
Shaftesbury, Lord......................................65, 66, 68
Sheepcote Road...145
Shops – A.J. Abbot, cobblers...................................91
    Adams Furniture Stores........................102, 103
    W.J. Barnard, menswear 94
    The Bazaar, photographic materials 96
    Boots, chemists................................83, 84, 90
    J. Brazier, dairymen......................................100
    Brentnall & Cleland, coal merchants 86
    Broadway Lending Library................................92
    R. Burns (formerly Chathams) 79
    Capels, opticians.....................................88, 89
    Leonard Cave, sports outfitters........................92
    W.H. Cullen, grocers................................87, 93
    Feltons, music store 92
    Freeman, Hardy & Willis, shoes..................90, 93
    A.S. Ginger, butcher 98
    Edmund Goshawk, bird stuffer 82
    Grange Furnishing Stores................................90
    C.J. Gueran, confectioner 99
    F. Gurney, grocer & wine merchant...................96
    Hinchcliffe's, coal merchants 88
    Harvey & Shillingford, grocers..........................92
    Hedges, confectioners....................................95
    Home & Colonial, grocers 83, 90, 93
    H. Horrex, shoe-maker 99
    Jaques, stationers..95
    J. Lambert, cobbler 91
    Lidstones, butchers 81
    Lilley & Skinner, shoes 86
    Lyons Tea Shop 84
    Nanette's, dress shop 92
    H. Rigden, chemists (Greenhill Pharmacy).........88
    J. Sainsbury, grocers 26, 83, 84, 90, 93, 96, 100
    Sheppard's Book Shop 88
    Somerton's, dress shop 90
    Sopers (Debenhams), department store ..85, 86, 88, 92, 120, 121
    Sladden's, drapers 92, 94, 120
    G. Smith, newsagent......................................93
    R. Smith, riding boots 87
    Stiles Travelling Shop.....................................92
    Universal Stationers.......................................84
    Watney Combe Reid, brewery stores.................82
    Webbs, florists..88
    Wright Cooper, bakers 82

"Sometimes a Soldier" 200
South Hill Avenue..................................19, 76, 114
Stanmore Park..77
Stanmore Hill......................................49, 98, 126, 184
Stanmore Post Office...184
Stations –
    Alperton 21
    Belmont 12, 22
    Harrow on the Hill................................13, 17, 24
    Hatch End 10, 11
    Harrow & Wealdstone 8, 9, 11, 24, 52, 86, 120
    North Harrow 18
    Northwick Park...17
    Rayners Lane.......................................37, 38, 41
    South Harrow 14, 19, 20, 24
    Stanmore..14, 22
Station Road, Harrow 15, 78, 81-85, 88, 90, 92, 104, 105, 107, 112, 120, 144, 186, 188, 190
Station Road, Wealdstone..................................161
Stogden, The Rev. Edgar 69, 199
Stuart, J.N. 197
Stuart Road, Wealdstone 58, 59
Sudbury Common 176
Sudbury Court Road..29
Sudbury Hill 44
Sudbury Pest House 176
Suffolk Road, Harrow 39
Syon House..131

Tauber, Richard 114
Thornton, Percy M 192
"The Times"...163
Tipping family 104
Trollope, Anthony 25
Tyburn Lane 74

University of Westminster 78

Victoria Hall, Harrow 145
Vine Cottages...176

Wallace, Nellie 114
Warren House, Stanmore 195, 198
Watford Road..29, 78, 158, 182
Watson, Maud & Lillian 154
Weald Lane, Harrow Weald 23
Waxwell Lane, Pinner...174
Wealdstone Fire Brigade 171, 173, 174
Wealdstone High Street 83, 93, 94, 103, 122, 196
Wealdstone Petty Sessions 108
Wealdstone Police Station..................................189
Wealdstone Swimming Pool 161
Weissmuller, Johnny 160
Wembley Hight Road 109, 185
Wembley Post Office 185
Wembley Swimming Pool 162
West Street...81, 118, 165, 188, 190
West Street Police Station 188, 189
Whitcombe, Rev. Guy 201
Whittington Way 39
Wightman Cup 157
Wilde, Oscar...54, 180
Wimbledon Tennis Championships 152
Wolfit, Sir Donald 114
Wolseley Road, Wealdstone................................106
Wolstenholme, Sir John 136
Woodbridge, James...184
Woolley, Rev. Geoffrey 200